DEVELOPMENT ECONOMICS

Development Economics

A New Paradigm

SYED NAWAB HAIDER NAQVI

Sage Publications
New Delhi/Newbury Park/London

First published in 1993 by

Sage Publications India Pvt Ltd
M-32 Greater Kailash Market I
New Delhi 110 048

Sage Publications Inc	**Sage Publications Ltd**
2455 Teller Road	6 Bonhill Street
Newbury Park, California 91320	London EC2A 4PU

Published by Tejeshwar Singh for Sage Publications India Pvt Ltd, phototypeset by Vijaya Enterprises, Madras, and printed at Chaman Enterprises, Delhi.

Library of Congress Cataloging-in-Publication Data

Naqvi, Syed Nawab Haider.
    Development economics: a new paradigm / Syed Nawab Haider Naqvi.
       p.   cm.
    Includes bibliographical references and index.
    1. Economic development. I. Title.
HD82. N265   1993   338.9—dc20   92-40700

ISBN : 81-7036-328-4 (India – hbk)
        0-8039-9469-9 (U.S. – hbk)
        81-7036-329-2 (India – pbk)
        0-8039-9470-2 (U.S. – pbk)

Dedicated
to
my wife, Saeeda,
and to our daughters,
Andalib, Tehmina, Qurratulain
and Neelofar

Contents

Contents

Foreword

Apart from some notable exceptions in Asia, developing countries languished during the decade of the eighties. They were weighed down by a deteriorating external economic environment marked by debt burdens, shrinking resource flows, rising protectionist trends and falling commodity prices. For many of them, the decade of the eighties was indeed a 'lost decade'. The weakening external economic environment was, unhappily, accompanied by a virtual collapse of the North–South dialogue. The focus of attention shifted instead to the domestic policies of developing countries. Domestic 'adjustment' became the key prescription for these countries during the eighties with its advocacy of a liberal policy stance in the direction of deregulation, export orientation, privatisation and freedom for market forces. All these found their way into the package of conditions governing aid and assistance.

These developments were matched by fresh thinking in the realm of economic theory. A school of neo-classical economics came into prominence which advocated free-market policies and denounced state intervention. One of the victims of this thinking was 'development economics' with the role it ascribed to the state in guiding the development process and its concern for attaining social goals. Development economics was pronounced dead not only by its detractors but also by some of its early adherents. The rise to prominence of these arguments and the policies based on them were not accompanied by any general revitalisation of the development process. At the same time, they reduced confidence both in the role of the state and in the conscious pursuit of equity and social justice at the national level and in development cooperation internationally.

The time has come to face this challenge and this is the task Professor Naqvi has set for himself in this volume. He starts with the question 'Is development economics a paradigm with a "territory" of its own?' Professor Naqvi answers with a vigorous 'Yes'. While development economics has its roots in mainstream economics, it also has a particular identity. The author lays bare the weaknesses of the free-market theory and one of its basic premises, the 'Pareto-optimality' principle, as guides to development policy. But he insists at the same time that development economics must itself evolve and take on new dimensions which are well-founded in rational analysis. It must not fight shy of a normative content and should justifiably take pride in its commitment to growth with distributive justice and the redress of social problems. Professor Naqvi sets out the theoretical foundations of his argument and concludes that: 'To ensure growth with equity, development economics should continue with its perception of a "mixed economy", whereby the government and the market are needed to help initiate and sustain the development process.' Single-minded devotion to the free-market ideology and the neglect of distributional issues will fail in practice if only because its conceptual foundations are incomplete.

Professor Naqvi's study is comprehensive in its scope. He deals with various schools of thought and provides in the process rich and fascinating comments on economic thinking, both past and present, on development issues. But he does much more than that for, in analysing the shortcomings and needs of development theory, he makes his own valuable contribution to the evolution of development economics itself. All this he does in a style that attracts attention for its lucidity, rigour and liveliness. Professor Naqvi's book is important and timely. It should contribute to the launching of a new phase marked both by national policies that are forged in the context of the social, political and economic realities of developing countries, and by a renewed commitment to international cooperation for development.

GAMANI COREA
Colombo
June 1992

PREFACE

Forty years after having come into existence, development economics is widely accepted, although it lacks universal acclaim. Despite some pessimistic evaluations of the subject, the academic community has granted it the right to a separate existence. This recognition has not been easily won. From the first full-length evaluation of the discipline by Chenery (1965), which regards it as a variation on the classical theme of comparative advantage, to Stern's sympathetic review of the contributions that the discipline has made to the state of economic knowledge (1989), development economics has experienced many a vicissitude—both the laurels of glory and the 'arrows of outrageous fortune'. Finally, it has become an industry in its own right. Not only the social profitability of this industry but also its 'private' profitability appears to be strictly positive; for instance, the publishing industry continues to patronize it and publish full-length books on the subject. Four decades of development experience, the production of massive cross-country and time-series data about a large number of development variables, the construction of large macroeconomic models and fast-running computers and the application of mathematical methods have all combined to lay the foundations of a theoretically rigorous and policy-relevant development paradigm, which is gradually replacing the old one.[1] All this is good news for development economists, who can now afford not only bread but also some butter for their daily parsnips.

However, as Newton's Third Law of Motion has taught us, 'to every Action there is always opposed and equal Reaction'. Thus, quite expectedly, the agnostics (the so-called 'liberals') have stepped up their (intellectual) 'reactionary' activities in direct proportion to the gains made by development economics. The *étatisme* implied strongly by some of the earlier development doctrines — for example, 'balanced (unbalanced) growth', the 'big-push', 'minimum critical effort'—is considered by them not only to be the indelible birthmark of the sub-discipline, but also as having defined its entire personality once and for all. Thus, a proof—indeed, *any* proof—of the efficiency of the free market is taken as a decisive refutation of development economics [Harberler (1988)]. Not only on the pages of textbooks and scientific journals, but also in the real world — for instance, in Eastern Europe, the erstwhile Soviet Union, China, Japan, Southeast Asia — market forces are seen to be defeating development economics [Crook (1989); Little (1982)].

Fortunately, there is nothing to support such conclusions concerning the demise, actual or predicted, of our discipline. In particular, there is not much circumstantial evidence to warrant the charge that development economics 'constitutes in itself a major obstacle to development in backward regions' [Walters (1989)]. In fact, those developing countries where development economics is taught, have grown reasonably fast (for instance, Pakistan, India), while some others have done so very fast (for example, South Korea). On the other hand, in the developing countries of Eastern Europe and the erstwhile Soviet Union, where the state-controlled political system has broken down in recent times, development economics has been neither taught nor practised. Indeed, there is every reason to believe that the economic systems of these crisis-ridden ccuntries may not have been helped at all by the talismanic quackery of supply-side economics.

Thus, development economics, as a discipline in its own right, is in no danger of evaporating under the heat of liberalist ideas. It is a fact, however, that in many vital aspects it is not what it used to be in the fifties, mainly because it is undergoing a dynamic process of consolidation and change. To complicate matters further, it is not at all clear which direction the next cycle of development of our discipline will take. It is, therefore, a worthwhile enterprise— which this volume undertakes —to reassure ourselves about the inner strength of development economics and its funda- mental purpose. The basic question in this context is: Is development economics a paradigm with a territory of its own?

Interpreting the word 'paradigm' broadly as a distinct weltanschauung, the answer to this question must be in the affirmative. This is the central theme of this book. Develop- ment economics is presented in these pages not as a deviant branch of mainstream economics, deserving the treatment reserved for heretics, but as a subject performing a role that mainstream economics is unwilling to play—to acquire an understanding of the vital problems that developing economies typically face, and to offer sensible remedies to resolve them. It also digs deeper than mainstream economics because to deal with economic problems such as the alleviation of poverty, it must not only encompass positivistic goals but also make normative judgements. And, partly due to its somewhat 'natural' preoccupation with development issues, it cannot afford to be irrevocably wedded to the market. All this amounts to asserting that development economics offers an approach to development issues which is different from mainstream economics; indeed, it has a different set of research priorities. For this very reason, the problematic it deals with is wider than the theory of economic growth. Rather than being engrossed with economic efficiency and steady-state solutions, it is concerned primarily with processes that tend to raise the per capita income and distribute it more equitably. If such an assertion of autonomy sins against the 'unity' and universality of the discipline of economics, then this is not a decisive argument against our discipline nor a final call for it to rejoin the mother-ship, that is, neo-classical economics. Instead, this assertion offers a sobering thought about the essential relativity of economics vis-a-vis the nature of society.[2]

However, a declaration of autonomy is not necessarily a rejection of mainstream economics. In particular, we cannot claim that growth theory, which is essentially an inter-temporal investigation of the static general-equilibrium theory,[3] is totally irrelevant to development economics. Indeed, there is a large body of growth literature which is directly relevant to development economics. For instance, the theory of optimal control is useful in understanding the inter-temporal character of investment decisions — for instance, in determining the optimal size of savings, in estimating the required amount of foreign aid, in making long-term development plans.[4] One may even make a stronger statement and claim that the relative neglect of growth theory in particular, and of general-equilibrium economics in general, has been, on balance, counter-productive for the growth of development economics. The failure of development economics to assign crucial roles

16

in the process of growth to technological change and to human capital, its tendency to overemphasize savings as a means to raise the growth of output on a permanent basis, the rather tentative nature of its main hypotheses, as well as the relative unconcern of its practitioners with achieving the rigour, generality, and simplicity of general-equilibrium economics can be cited as examples of such neglect.[5]

But for development economics to seek intellectual help from neo-classical economics is not necessarily the same as losing its own distinct identity—especially when such a self-sacrifice is both unnecessary and undesirable. This is because, by virtue of its broad purpose and basic thrust, mainstream economics, and especially growth theory, does not help either in fully understanding the nature of the development problem or in diagnosing any meaningful remedial policies.[6] General-equilibrium economics cannot address the basic problems of development economics by pursuing its 'ideologically-free' scientific ideal. More specifically, the Pareto-optimality criterion, which is efficiency-oriented to an 'antiseptic' extent and is an integral component of the neoclassical prescription, cannot be utilised to comprehend the dimensions of the development problem adequately. Status quoist by temperament, this alchemic rule would not inform us that the basic problem of economic development is to secure economic growth and achieve an equitable distribution of income.[7] It certainly would not help in grasping the importance of changing the structure of private-property holdings in society to improve the lot of the least privileged. Furthermore, the make-believe neo-classical world of self-clearing markets blessed with full employment, does not even recognize the phenomenon of unemployment, let alone offer any remedies for it.[8] Indeed, there is an intrinsic tendency in the neo-classical tradition to blame unemployment on the voluntary actions of wage-earners; and sometimes even to dismiss the problem by treating practically any level

17

of actual unemployment as the 'natural' rate of unemployment, about which nothing can or should be done.

A full-time preoccupation with self-clearing markets also leads mainstream economics of the Walrasian vintage to consider the government as an 'outsider' whose intervention can only make matters worse.[9] But the development economist cannot afford the luxury of such *anarchic* ideas; he has to remember that for handling key development issues the proper institutional framework is that of a 'mixed' economy, in which both the private and the public sectors have mutually supportive roles to play. While in routine cases, free markets are the most suitable institutions to optimize output and maximize consumers' welfare, an activist role for the state is also fairly well-defined, especially in the Prisoner's Dilemma-type situation. In this, a public good, characterised by non-exclusivity and indivisibility, must be produced, in activities which create substantial external economies, or a structural change involving the redistribution of private property rights (as, for instance, in land reforms) must be made, or, at the initial stages of economic development, large amounts of investment resources are required to initiate and diversify the growth process — in all these and in similar situations, state intervention could be welfare-raising even if, subject to factors like the economic development of a particular society, the questions regarding its form and extent may remain open to debate.

To assert, as some economists do, that the market can be fruitfully relied upon even to effect a structural change provided private property rights are properly defined, is perhaps to stretch one's credulity a little. Indeed, it can be shown that in no case does a Pareto-optimal solution necessarily bespeak a market-oriented ideology [Debreu (1987)].[10] It is neither the most efficient solution, nor even the most equitable [Arrow (1979)]. The stock argument that 'government failure' is even more severe than market failure ignores cases where, due to the essentially 'asymmetric' nature of information available to rival economic agents, the efficiency of market outcomes cannot be guaranteed in advance [Akerlof (1970)]. When such a situation prevails, there may be no basis for choosing on a priori grounds between an allegedly inefficient government and an ill-informed market. Furthermore, such an argument is myopically focused on efficiency considerations alone [Stigler (1965)]; it leaves out of account issues of equity as relatively, if not absolutely, unimportant. But the case for government intervention is the strongest when such equity considerations *are* important—for instance, in facing up to the problem of poverty. Indeed, in this case, defining private property rights too firmly in the initial situation will make it impossible to embark on any programme of structural change. For instance, in such an eventuality, feudalism will be sanctified on a permanent basis.[11]

One of the apparently more attractive anti-*dirigistic* arguments is that the government ought to fail because the free market is the best preserver of individual liberty, which is accorded priority over all else. But this is by no means conclusive argument for the innate superiority of the markets. Only if it is decided in advance, presumably on ideological grounds, that the market does not interfere with individual liberty while the government invariably does, and only if individual liberty, especially with respect to private property rights, must be preserved even when it entails tolerating the worst kind of inequalities of income and wealth, does it follow that the market-based solutions will be, by definition, superior to any type of government intervention. Whatever be the justification for entertaining such arguments—or we may even call them tautologies—in mainstream economics, they cannot be acceptable to a development economist because economic development is ultimately

19

about readjusting the loci of economic power in order to promote economic growth with distributive justice. Of course, individual liberty must be prized as an absolute value, but not to the extent where preserving it means tolerating and perpetuating extreme social injustice and misery where the majority of mankind is concerned. This cannot be, even when Buchanan's 'calculus of consent' signals unanimity about such an undesirable state of affairs, or even if the rectification of such injustice offends Nozickian non-consequentialism.

One of the more important reasons why a neo-classical prescription fails to help is that, especially in the context of economic development, it becomes more difficult to distinguish between the 'is-questions' and the 'ought-questions'.[12] Answering such a complex set of questions involves making normative judgements, even interpersonal welfare comparisons. Thus, for instance, the self-interest maximization rule—'business as usual' even in the darkest hour—which mainstream economics has created in its own image, cannot be the sole index of rationality in thinking about such issues. Even though it is helpful in producing neat theoretical results, this rule is definitely not a universal description of actual or ideal human behaviour.[13] The rule becomes even more grotesque when it seeks to drive out of circulation everything that is not self-interest maximization, on the ground that it must by definition be irrational. The fact of the matter is that a significant part of our behaviour is motivated by altruism, even by commitment, and we may be willing to sacrifice some of our personal welfare for the benefit of others. The collective mind of mankind may regard such an event as economically beneficial, even though it may not be Pareto-optimal. What is even more important is that ethical considerations, based on either secular or religious motivations, focus our attention on crucial development concerns, such as, poverty, distributional inequities, and unemployment, with an urgency that positive economics lacks.[14]

A strictly neo-classical answer to development questions is also inadequate, partly because such an answer professes strict 'neutrality' regarding issues of justice in the economy. Indeed, according to Debreu (1991), economists would be required to take an 'inhuman stance' when confronted with such a choice.[15] It is in the nature of a positivistic calculus that it cannot even distinguish between a wealthy individual and a poor one, so that any redistributive scheme may as well be a perverse one—one that transfers from the poor to the rich.[16] It follows that development economics needs, among other things, a set of decision rules which explicitly allow normative judgements—for example, 'what would I do if I were in anyone else's shoes?'—to be able to prescribe institutional change where an undesirable status quo exists. Obviously, the Pareto-optimality rule underlying neo-classical economics is not of help, partly because it is inherently status quoist, and partly because it has not been programmed to answer value-loaded questions.[17] On the other hand, the Rawlsian criterion should be helpful because of its uncompromising insistence on satisfying the needs of the least-privileged individuals in society and on changing social and economic institutions if this cannot be done with the existing ones.[18] Of course, to become a true criterion of equality, the Rawlsian criterion needs to be suitably modified by a sensible rule which stipulates decreasing the number of the poor in selected states of the economy and imposing limits on what the rich receive. The important point is that it does raise the kind of questions which are helpful in conceptualizing development issues, and in suggesting adequate remedies for them.

It should be clear to the reader by now that this book is not always motivated by concerns that are universally shared by the profession of economists, or even by many development economists. Development economics in these pages does not appear as a 'rock of positivity', heartlessly concerned with the problems of growth alone. Instead, it is also seen as concerned with situations in which the need to make explicit normative judgements is too pressing to be ignored even at a theoretical level. Furthermore, I do not share the pessimistic view of those who have been writing obituary notices for development economics because some of its original insights, for instance, the balanced-growth doctrine, the vent-for-surplus conjecture, the centre-periphery hypothesis, and the pioneers-latecomers syndrome, may not be as fashionable or as relevant today as in their heyday in the fifties, or because its earlier *étatistic* leanings may now have become suspect. Similarly, I differ with those who think that to be able to face up to difficult development problems like poverty, development economics should fall in love with the free market. Finally, I reject the viewpoint that development economics is some brand of applied economics,[19] that it is not a discipline in its own right or that it is blighted by the poverty of its ideas. Instead, this book emphasizes the utility of our discipline by referring to its paradigmatic character and ethical nature, and its mixed-economy orientation.

Even a cursory reading of this book should make it clear that I have some definite notions about which ideas from mainstream economics are helpful for the healthy growth of development economics as a new intellectual paradigm, which will provide an understanding of reality in the developing countries and help to not only explain this reality but also, if need be, to change it. One does not have to be a Marxist to insist that an essential building block for a useful development theory is an overarching vision about socio-economic change leading to a more just social order, in which the needs of the least-privileged sections in society are looked after in the best possible fashion, where unemployment, inequitable distribution of income and wealth, extreme poverty, and social degradation are seen as problem areas deserving the highest priority in a programme for change, and in which human freedom is incomplete without some measure of equality. In short, following Meade, I believe that development economics should be inspired by 'a passionate desire to devise a better domestic and international society' [Meade (1983), p.268].

I have no doubt that such a vision of a better world can best be approximated in a democratic society with a mixed economy. According to T.H. Marshall (1950) such a society is simply an extension of the revolutionary eighteenth-century idea of the rights of the citizen. Such a welfare-oriented society could be labelled Keynesian or neo-Keynesian—involving as it does a restriction of free markets and the creation of an effective system of transfer from the rich to the poor. On the other hand, the Friedmanite, Hayekian, rational-expectationist, supply-side, and neo-classical political-economy visions are all examples of misleading labels for development economics. Also, the 'bloody-mindedness' of some of our pioneers with respect to the growth objective, and their apparent lack of concern about distribution and ethical issues, is not a heritage worth preserving in the next cycle of the growth of our discipline. Economic growth is clearly the vehicle of economic development, but, at the same time, an equitable distribution of the fruits of economic progress is necessary to make the entire exercise worthwhile for the majority of the population. This point was made most forcefully by one of the pioneers of development economics, Tinbergen (1959; 1977).

I firmly believe that the new-found infatuation with unadulterated capitalism, made respectable by reference to questionable circumstantial and empirical evidence, that is, the remarkable growth performance of the East Asian countries and the collapse of the East European socialist regimes, does not provide such a vision.[20] Indeed, such ideas are against the progressive design of history, and they have done great damage to Western democracies by robbing them of their humane character and by making the privileged class both stronger and more insensitive to human suffering. The rise of unemployment to unprecedented levels in the post-war era is directly attributable to the intermediation of Laffer curves, rational expectations and Friedmanite monetarism. It has led to social instability in these societies which have gained very little in terms of economic efficiency. I am apprehensive that *the transplantation of such defective ideas onto the fragile social structures of the developing countries will have even more undesirable consequences, not only for equity but also for growth.* It is clearly an unsatisfactory social philosophy which, in the process of securing individual freedom for the few, deprives us of our compassion towards the withered lives of countless millions, and which, in the pursuit of economic efficiency, is incapable of providing answers to such obvious questions as those of poverty and unemployment. On the other hand, a satisfactory social philosophy would emphasize entitlements as much as achievements.

This volume consists of revised and updated versions of the Presidential Addresses that I have given every year since 1984 at the Annual General Meetings of the Pakistan Society of Development Economists, and which were later published in *The Pakistan Development Review.* At places, the revisions made have been quite extensive in order to present the argument in a more formal manner, to avoid unnecessary overlapping between what were different lectures delivered over a period of seven years, and to highlight the thematic continuity underlying the book. The repetition that remains is based on the idea that I try to discuss at length, in each successive chapter, what was only hinted at previously, and some issues which were analyzed in detail in a previous chapter are summarized in a subsequent lecture in order to keep the narrative as self-contained as possible. Thus, the paradigm of development economics is introduced in the first chapter, but it is fully developed only in the seventh chapter, taking into account the various building blocks of a useful development theory as identified in the intervening chapters. The themes discussed several times in these chapters, for example, the Pareto-optimality criterion and the Rawlsian principle, have been re-examined from a different angle each time so as to throw some fresh light on the surrounding 'territory'. I hope that this book, though it may well raise a lot of dust for joining issue with even the stalwarts of the discipline, may make many intricate development issues a little clearer. To this end, I have also tried to make these lectures more readable and thus accessible to a wider audience, but, I hope, not by sacrificing the analytical rigour or the accuracy of the argument. The review of a large body of literature having a direct and indirect bearing on development economics and the fairly comprehensive reference list placed at the end of the book should be a bonus to the students of the subject.

In revising these lectures for publication, I have benefited greatly from the comments by Mr Ghulam Ishaq Khan, now President of Pakistan, to whom I remain deeply indebted. I am most grateful to Dr Gamani Corea for contributing a Foreword to this volume, to Professor Lawrence Klein, Professor M. Ali Khan, and to an anonymous referee for their invaluable suggestions for improving the text of these lectures, and to Dr V. Kanesalingam for his general support. The advice of many participants at the Annual General Meetings of the Pakistan Society of Development Economists has also been helpful. In this connection, special mention must be made of Professors Edmond Malinvaud, Mahmood Hasan Khan, Pan Yotopolous, Peter Cornelisse, Suleiman Cohen, Ismail Sirageldin, John Mellor, Vernon Ruttan, and Ansley Coale. Professor Jan Tinbergen has also been kind enough to comment on some of these lectures in their original form. I have also benefited a great deal from the pioneering work of A. K. Sen on public choice theory. I am most grateful to Professor Alamgir Hashmi for making many editorial improvements. Mr Rana Mukhtar Ahmad has carefully prepared the final typescript. But, as always, the author alone is responsible for any inadequacies and errors that still remain.

NOTES

[1]By far the most valuable contribution has been made by the World Bank in the form of several yearly statistical publications. Most worthy of mention among these are *TIDE (Trends in Developing Economies), SID (Social Indicators of Development)*, and WDI (World Development Indicators).

[2]Deane (1983) has emphasized the 'relativity' of the discipline of economics: 'There is no one kind of truth which holds the key to the fruitful analysis of all economic problems, no pure economic theory that is immune to changes in social values or current policy problems' (p. 11).

[3]This opinion, held by Hahn (1987), is not widely shared. See, especially, Goodwin (1990).

[4]See Chakravarty (1969) for an example of the application of the theory of optimal control to problems of development policy. However, it may also be pointed out that it is by its application to development problems that some of these esoteric mathematical tools become relevant to economics.

[5]On the other hand, the estrangement between mainstream economics and development economics has also been detrimental to the former. Quite satisfied with its static existence, mainstream economics has not alluded frequently enough to its own origins—an understanding of the causes of the growth of the 'wealth of nations'. I agree with Sen (1988) that 'Development economics... has to be concerned not only with protecting its "own" territory, but also with keeping alive the foundational motivation of the subject of economics in gencral [i.e., development]' (p. 11).

[6]Hahn (1987) clearly states the reasons why 'neoclassical growth theory is not...even a theory of growth' (p. 625).

[7]However, the rule could be used to compute shadow prices for evaluating the efficiency of alternative investment plans.

[8]It is unfortunate that the recognition granted to this phenomenon by Keynesian economics at the macro level has been withdrawn of late by the rational-expectationists. The latter deny the possibility of reducing unemployment through macroeconomic management.

[9]However, this remark does not apply to the Akerlof-Stiglitz version of neo-classical economics. See, for instance, Stiglitz (1988).

26

[10]Debreu (1987) clearly states that the Pareto criterion is 'ideologically-free'. It could be used to demonstrate the 'unqualified superiority of the market economies', as well as to show that it really supports state intervention because of the 'discrepancies between the theoretic model and the economies they (i.e., economists) observe' (p. 402).

[11]It has been argued in the literature that governments ultimately serve the interests of vested interests, and may be thus incapable of bringing about reforms of the kind noted in the text. [Becker (1983)]. This is, no doubt, true to some extent; for instance, the relative failure of the governments in Pakistan, India and the Philippines to carry out meaningful land reforms. But there are also instances where the more development-oriented governments have succeeded in bringing about structural reforms, such as, South Korea and Taiwan. There is nothing inherent in government per se that makes it incapable of promoting structural change; it depends on the type of government in question. Furthermore, it needs to be pointed out that all democratic governments—indeed, even undemocratic ones— are subjected to constant public pressure to display 'concrete' achievements for the benefit of the poor. In many cases such pressures do succeed. In Pakistan, the first really effective land reforms were carried out by the military regime of Ayub Khan. [See Naqvi et al. (1989)].

[12]For details, see Putnam (1990).

[13]Indeed, as pointed out by Machlup (1956), the profit maximization rule, based on self-interest, is empirically non-verifiable.

[14]In the United States, the recent Pastoral Letter (1985) has highlighted important economic issues on moral grounds. Interestingly enough, high-brow economists like Tobin (1985) and Klein (1985) have supported the Letter: 'The Catholic Bishops have put the present economic debate on a new plane'(p. 364).

[15]Debreu (1991) advocates such an 'inhuman stance', whereby economists 'must be impartial spectators of a play in which they are the actors' (p. 8).

[16]This is because the ordinalist calculus underlying much of mainstream economics does not allow the interpersonal comparison of utilities, and welfare is measured exclusively in terms of the metric of utilities.

[17]The distributive neutrality of the Pareto-optimality rule is not in the least diminished by the possibility of making lumpsum income transfers from the potential gainers to the potential losers. This is partly because the loss suffered by one (poor) person cannot be morally justified by the gain enjoyed of another (rich) person.

[18]It is instructive to note that the apparently 'secular' Rawlsian criterion is directly related to the Judaeo-Christian ethical principle of helping the

Development Economics

'powerless'. [See the Pastoral Letter (1985)]. Islamic ethical principles also accord priority to the needs of the 'oppressed' and the 'deprived'. [See Naqvi (1981)..Iqbal (1986)].

[19] A recent evaluation of the subject refers to development economics as a 'branch of applied economics' [Bell (1987), p.825].

[20] Heilbroner's (1990) recent evaluation falls in this unacceptable category. He asserts: 'with few exceptions, socialism has experienced a public delegitimization... whereas capitalism, despite its failures, has enjoyed...a rising degree of internal political support' (p.1097). In my opinion, it is too soon to infer that the rejection of undemocratic socialist regimes implies nothing but an unbounded love for unfettered capitalism.

1

Development Economists
in the Emperor's
New Clothes

This may not be the worst of times for the discipline of development economics, but it is not the best of times either. The discipline, for all its internal strength, is gripped by a kind of schizophrenia. While development economics is accepted generally, it is not always given a warm reception in either the academic or the policy-making circles. This is partly because the consensus of the fifties and the sixties about the nature and legitimacy of the discipline and its world-view have been seriously strained. The search is on for a new consensus about the purpose and scope of development economics.

Thus, to set the record straight, and to acquire a modicum of self-assurance, the central question that we must now address ourselves to is: Are the development economists wearing the 'emperor's new clothes'? If, as some economists assert, they are, then we are in danger of losing our identity as intellectuals armed with a cause, a technique, and a special message. Were that the case at all, then, being rational profit-maximizers, we had better return to the so-called mainstream, or, in other words, (neo-classical) economics and, at best, function as a branch of applied economics.

Fortunately, however, this is *not* the case. This lecture and the following ones in this volume are designed to show the reason why.

OBITUARY NOTICES FOR DEVELOPMENT ECONOMICS

It would be instructive to start our narrative by considering the words of Schultz (1964), who denies not only the existence but also the very need of a 'separatist' development economics. In his Nobel Lecture (1981), he claims that 'standard economic theory is as applicable to the scarcity problems that confront the low-income countries as to the corresponding problems of the high-income countries' for the simple reason that 'poor people are no less concerned about improving their lot and that of their children than rich people are'. Besides, he points out, 'the early economists dealt with conditions [in Western Europe] similar to those prevailing in low-income countries today'. The failure to see such a simple point has been, according to Schultz, the 'original sin' of development economists. Since history, logic, and simple common sense are against development economics, it would be only rational for its practitioners to give up and opt for mainstream economics, both for a better conceptualization of the development problem and for offering sensible policy advice. This opinion is shared by Haberler (1988), Bauer (1972), Little (1982), and Walters (1989). On the other hand, there are many others, such as, Lewis (1984), Sen (1983), Chenery (1988; 1989), Stern (1989), who would argue the opposite.

As if shaken by this state of schizophrenic confusion, Hirschman (1981b) wrote what could be regarded as an obituary for our discipline. Somewhat wistfully, he declared: 'I cannot help feeling that the old liveliness is not there, that new ideas are ever harder to come by and that the field is not adequately reproducing itself', so that 'the decline of development economics cannot be fully reversed'. Accordingly, he counsels fellow economists to bear the passage philosophically because 'we may have gained in maturity what we have lost in excitement'.

In order to think clearly about the nature and significance of development economics, I have examined both these arguments in the present volume. In this chapter, we may evaluate the claims made by Schultz and Hirschman.

Schultz's Iconoclasm

The difficulty with Schultz's argument is that his case against the existence of development economics rests entirely on the assertion that farmers are rational decision-makers, who respond positively to monetary and non-monetary in-centives.[1] Now, to reject development economics on the basis of a single refutation is not good logic because, in the stochastic world of economics, the improbability of a hypo-thesis does not imply that it is false, and even the demonstration of the falsity of just one element in a doctrine, which is a collection of hypotheses, cannot invalidate the entire doctrine. To put the same point positively, the mere demonstration that *one* assumption of the standard economic theory does hold for developing countries does not imply that *all* its assumptions must also hold. At any rate, it has never been seriously claimed that irrational decision-making is a regular feature of economic agents in underdeveloped economies, even if certain allusions to this effect may have been made by some economists when development economics was still a new discipline.

The historical part of Schultz's argument is also questionable. The fact that West European countries in an earlier stage of their development experienced problems similar to those of the underdeveloped countries of the Third World today does not necessarily invalidate the case for development economics. Even if it is assumed that the nature of the economic challenge then was the same as it is now, it does not follow that the quality and intensity of the 'response' of the Third World today must be identical to that of the developing countries of the West in the nineteenth century. Nor does it follow that the prescriptions of development economists must be identical to those of the classical economics of Adam Smith and Ricardo, even if their work bears a faint resemblance to the classical economics of the eighteenth and nineteenth centuries. As discussed in the next lecture, what is an anachronism in the West today may not have current relevance in today's developing countries. It is for this reason that Gerschenkron (1962) jeered at the Rostowian prescription that 'the process of industrialization repeated itself from country to country lumbering through his [i.e., Rostow's] pentametric rhythm'. Instead, Gerschenkron insisted on the multiplicity of growth paths, depending on the special circumstances, policies, and ideologies of different developing countries. For

> in a number of historical instances industrialization processes, when launched at length in a backward country, showed considerable differences, as compared with more advanced countries, not only with regard to the speed of development (the rate of industrial growth) but also with regard to the productive and organizational structures of industry which emerged from those processes.

Hirschman's Obituary

According to Hirschman (1981b), when it all began in the early fifties, development economics was essentially raised on the simultaneous rejection by development economists of the 'mono-economics' claim and the assertion of the 'mutual-benefit' claim. The alleged rejection of the mono-economics claim by economists like Nurkse (1953), Rosenstein-Rodan (1943), Lewis (1954), Leibenstein (1957), and many others, and their insistence on the need for a new economics was based on the existence of rural underemployment in developing countries and on the fact that these countries, which suffered from the late-comer's syndrome, needed a different kind of treatment in the form of a 'big push', 'great spurt', 'minimum critical effort', 'take-off', 'backward and forward linkages', etc. On the other hand, the acceptance of the 'mutual-benefit' claim rested on the belief that there existed an essential harmony of interest between the developed and the developing countries. The former felt capable of helping the latter move out of underdevelopment through financial assistance. According to Hirschman, since these two claims are no longer acceptable, it is necessary to resolve the seeming stalemate between the thesis put forward by the founding fathers of the discipline and the antithesis propounded by those who succeeded them by presenting a grand new synthesis. However, as he asserts, 'no new synthesis appeared'. Hence the obituary notice, which appears to have been somewhat premature. Indeed, this line of argument is faulty, because the development of a science in response to the endogenous and exogenous shocks involving a reformulation, even rejection, of some of its original hypothesis is not a sign of its decay—on the contrary, it is an indication of robust health.

The main problem with Hirschman's argument is that he has put development economics in a typological cell, in which it may not belong. The fact is that, with a few honourable exceptions like Hirschman (1958) and Bauer (1972), the mutual-benefit claim was never widely accepted by development economists. Prebisch (1959) and Singer (1952) rejected such a claim. They insisted that the two sets of countries were, instead, engaged in an antagonistic, zero-sum game. Further, there was Myrdal (1956a) who saw the mechanism of international trade as contributing, through the so-called 'backwash effect', to the growing inequality between nations. Lewis (1955) also held the view that without appropriate state intervention the developing countries with surplus labour would lose out to the developed countries, where labour's share tends to rise with the growth of national income.[2] Since then the doctrines of 'dependency' and 'unequal exchange', advocated by Cardoso (1972), Emmanuel (1972), Amin (1976), and others of the neo-Marxian band have questioned the veracity of the mutual-benefit claim.

There is an undeniable element of truth in the neo-Marxian thinking which should be acceptable to development economists who may not, however, like to be labelled 'neo-Marxian'.

For instance, the Kemp-Ohyama (1978) model highlights the fundamental asymmetry in the working of the international economic system which works against the South and is relatively more lenient to the North. This 'truth' is in no way invalidated by disproving the Prebisch-Singer thesis that the evidence about the alleged movement of terms of trade against the South is mixed [Spraos (1980)], or that many of the countries of the South now produce and export both primary goods and manufactured products [World Development Report (1991)]. The fact of the matter is that, as amply demonstrated by the Brandt Report (1980), when market power matters, those who have more gain more from trade than those who have less. Furthermore, the unequal-exchange syndrome poisons the relations not only between the developed and the developing countries, but also between different classes within most of the developing countries, where these classes are pitted against each other in serious conflict. Even apart from such broad sociological facts, there is the obvious conflict of interest in these countries between the agricultural and the urban sectors of the economy, where, as exemplified by the seesaw movement of the internal terms of trade, the farmer loses out to both landlords and urban dwellers in the competition for economic growth.

SEARCH FOR NEW FOUNDATIONS

To prove its right to a separate existence in economics, development economics cannot but respond to these facts of economic life. This assertion can be explored more fruitfully in terms of the methodology of the philosophy of science developed and applied of late by Popper (1980), Kuhn (1962), and Lakatos (1970). In their spirit, the question to ask is: Does development economics constitute a new 'paradigm', or more accurately, a new 'scientific research programme'? Does it consist of a distinctive set of metaphysical beliefs about how the economic universe hangs together, as well as a number of refutable hypotheses about the behaviour of economic agents in this universe? Furthermore, if such a scientific research programme does exist, is it theoretically and empirically 'progressive', in the sense of having a greater 'empirical content' than standard economic theory claims to possess? And, finally, does the new research programme predict 'novel facts' about the developing countries?[3] Some of these issues are discussed in greater detail in Chapters 2 and 7. For the present, a few illustrations will clarify the nature of these questions and demonstrate why the answers should be in the affirmative.

A clear indication of the 'paradigm shift' is the change in the focus of analysis from economic growth to economic development, with a view to comprehending better the changing objective reality on the ground. To some extent, standard growth theory did help to clarify some key aspects of the central problems that these countries faced. These insights relate basically to the role in the growth process that the Harrod-Domar model assigns to such variables as the propensity to save, the capital/output ratio, and the growth of population. Nevertheless, growth theory, notwithstanding such invaluable insights, has been concerned with esoteric issues which are not very relevant to development theory or policy in the developing countries—nor, indeed, in the developed countries. In particular, its almost full-time pre-occupation with elegant proofs of the existence and stability of steady-state growth paths has no operational content in it.[4] Only one example should suffice to illustrate this point: According to an estimate made by Sato (1963), the time taken by an economy which is off the steady-state path to get back on to it is about one hundred years! This is a literal example of the Keynesian long-run in which we shall all be dead. It is for such reasons that Hicks (1976) remarked that growth theory reflected no more than 'the shadows of the real problems'. (Respectable exceptions to this stricture are the theoretical and empirical studies initiated by Solow [1957]. It is in this context that we need a new, 'progressive', scientific research programme to deal with the real world's problems.

What are the main elements of the new scientific research programme that development economics represents?[5] First, compared to growth theory, development economics reflects a clearer realization that the process of economic development entails *structural change*—which, among other things, involves a distribution of assets and private property, particularly of landed property. This is not only socially just, but also economically efficient. For instance, Berry and Cline (1979) and Naqvi et al. (1989) show that agricultural productivity is negatively related to the large-size farm holdings that characterise a feudal structure.[6] Baran (1952) had also emphasized that, in order to release the forces of socio-economic change, the existing power structure, which represented a symbiosis of the worst elements of two modes of production, must be redesigned. In his words:

> This superimposition of business *mores* over ancient oppression by landed gentries resulted in compounded exploitation, more outrageous corruption and more glaring social injustice. (What resulted from this superimposition) was an economic and political amalgam combining the worst features of both the worlds—feudalism and capitalism—and blocking effectively all possibilities of economic growth.

These observations are a fairly accurate description of the conditions prevailing in some of the developing countries, including Pakistan, where the feudal-capitalistic structures compromise their growth potential and, at the same time,

37

restrict the flow of goods and services to the poor.[7] It is interesting to note that every developing country which has achieved economic success, such as, Japan and South Korea, had freed its economy from the chains of feudalism at the outset.

Second, the attempts to reconcile economic growth with the distribution of income to eradicate the worst forms of poverty in a manner that is socially and politically acceptable should feature prominently in the research programme of development economics.

The reality of the situation in developing countries made development economists fear that if significant direct income transfers were not made to the poor, any rapid economic growth that did take place might itself impede the process of structural change, by worsening the distribution of income and wealth and by impoverishing even further those living below the 'poverty line'. (The 'poverty line', it must be admitted, is drawn both differently and indifferently by various authors.) It was these factors that highlighted the need, particularly in the seventies, for a new development strategy. (See Chapter 2.)

A perfectly viable strategy for promoting capital accumulation in a socially desirable way would be to keep the rate of capitalist profit, adjusted for the share of wages in net output, at a level that could be realized in the production of wage goods. This level should then set the ceiling for the rate of profit in the rest of the economy. This is the essence of Sraffa's (1975) generalization of the Ricardian theory of determination of the rate of profit on investment, and it is of special relevance for developing countries. This is because these countries, for political and moral reasons, cannot ignore the dictates of social justice in their bid to secure high rates of economic growth. The important point, as I have noted, is that the theory of economic development deals explicitly with comprehensive social change, which cannot be analysed with the tools of standard economic theory alone.[8]

A philosophical reason, noted by Boulding (1966), for the inapplicability of standard economic theory to development problems is that, where knowledge is an essential part of the system, the knowledge about the system changes the system itself. This is particularly true of the developing countries, where the initial stock of knowledge about the existing economic systems is small to begin with, and the rate of economic progress is directly related to an increase in knowledge about the dynamics of growth in such countries. As such, development economics must not only take into account the objective reality on the ground, but also the change that occurs in this very reality. This is because it cannot assume the objective reality to have remained unchanged as information inputs are injected into the system.[9]

Third, the new scientific research programme that development economics represents explicitly repudiates, as it should, the assumptions of unchanging tastes and independence of individual's utility functions.[10] The restrictive nature of such assumptions, which are routinely made by neoclassical economists, should be transparent when it is remembered that the process of economic development itself represents, in the words of Samuel Johnson, 'the wild vicissitudes of tastes' and the preferences of the various strata of society in developing countries. Similarly, as Veblen (1973) and Duesenberry (1952) both observed fairly long ago, consumption functions are typically interdependent. This is particularly the case in developing countries. An interesting example of such interdependence is the conjecture by Hirschman-Rothschild (1973) that, in the early stages of development, growing inequalities of income are tolerated by the poor only in the hope that they too will ultimately receive a due share in the wealth of the nation, and that this tolerance of inequality diminishes sharply once the poor realize that their expectations will not be fulfilled.

It should be clear by now that development economics

constitutes a viable scientific research programme. It remains to be proven that this programme is also 'progressive' in that it has *'ample* empirical content', and that it predicts 'novel facts' about developing countries which are not comprehensible with the help of standard economic theory. It may be noted in this context that the most important theoretical and empirical advances in development economics have indeed been made in the process of examining changing reality in the developing countries. For instance, the recognition of surplus labour in rural areas as the key factor in developing countries led to the formulation of the model of 'rural under-employment' by Lewis (1955), which was elaborated by other economists like Fei and Ranis (1963). Later, the models of 'migration and unemployment' developed by Harris and Todaro (1970), and much improved and elaborated on by Khan (1980, 1987a), focused instead on urban unemployment, which is caused by rural-urban migration and a politically-determined urban wage. Another example of the ample empirical content of development economics is the spate of empirical work that has been generated on the relation between economic growth, income distribution and unemployment. These studies have resulted in the generation of new knowledge about the process of development. One such pioneering study, inspired solely by the actual problems of developing countries, is by Chenery et al. (1974), and there are many others. Yet another example of the theoretical and empirical progress that has been made principally as a consequence of studying the real situation of the developing countries is the theory of effective rates of protection, developed mainly by Johnson (1969), Bhagwati (1978), Balassa (1971), Corden (1966), and Krueger (1978). This theory spans a large body of empirical work, which, with the help of such 'operational' concepts as explicit and implicit effective rates of protection and domestic resource cost, throws new light on the industrialization strategies of developing countries

[Naqvi and Kemal (1991)]. This work has added to the empirical content of development economics, even though a lot of unnecessary theoretical elaborations have also been made in this area. For instance, the use of a non-observable Pareto-optimality criterion as a reference point for measuring the loss incurred due to the adoption of second-best policies has compromised the usefulness of the policy recommendations coming out of this work, which sometimes has degenerated into an ideological advocacy of competitive markets and free trade and a denunciation of state intervention in general.

These are just a few examples of the manner in which development economics has predicted novel facts, but many more such examples can be cited. It should be clear, then, that development economists, far from wearing the mythical 'Emperor's Clothes', have presentable clothes to dress themselves in. In any case, the important question to discuss is: What should development economists, including those in India and Pakistan, be doing in their distinguished raiments?

THE ROAD AHEAD

It may be useful at this point to anticipate some of the themes discussed in subsequent chapters. First, development economics must continue to focus, theoretically and empirically, on the relationship between economic growth and structural change. This is because even if the income of the poor is rising faster than the income of the rich, the absolute gap between the two will not even begin to narrow until the ratio of their respective wealth holdings equals the inverse ratio of the growth rates of their relative incomes. A redistribution of initial wealth holdings in developing countries is, therefore, essential to establish some kind of an 'optimum regime' wherein the gap between the rich and the poor is kept at a minimum. Tinbergen (1959) points out that 'as a rule the optimum requires income transfers' because at present the income differences between the rich and the poor are more unequal than is socially acceptable. Furthermore, empirically-oriented models like those of Chenery et al. (1974) should be constructed to make sure that, as economic growth proceeds apace—using both physical and human capital, the relative share of the poorest in the GNP does not fall. This latter condition must be met to prevent absolute poverty from getting any worse as a result of economic growth. In this connection, it is essential both that the GNP also account for 'bads' [Klein (1983)] and that it should be measured, by employing poverty weights and other devices, in a manner that accurately reflects the welfare-increasing content of economic growth. To this end, development economics should accord explicit recognition to the role of human capital in the process of economic development. This is a field in which Schultz (1970, 1981a); Becker (1964); Khan (1979) and Sirageldin (1966) have made useful contributions.

Second, to do its job efficiently, it is appropriate that development economics does not rely *exclusively* on Adam Smith's automatic price mechanism run by the Invisible Hand, though it ought not to repudiate it as irrelevant. (See Chapters 3 and 6). Leontief (1983) has noted that the efficiency and beneficence of the Invisible Hand, in accelerating economic growth, and raising labour's share in national product was never a fact.[11] It was indeed an illusion, sustained by the powerful waves of technological change that hit Western Europe with increasing intensity and frequency. However, Leontief warns that such a happy confluence of economic growth and income distribution will not hold, even in advanced countries, with the increasing importance of labour-saving computer technology which has permeated all sectors of developed economies. This happy confluence will be even more tenuous in developing countries where high rates of population growth keep real wages down, while the application of the Western computer technology tends to increase both rural underemployment and urban unemployment.

The central point raised in Leontief's assertion should be carefully noted by development economics: it is about the role of technological change in the process of economic development. (See Chapter 7). Cornwall (1977) has shown that in the spectacular growth episode of the post-war era which terminated in 1973, not more than half of the growth rates actually achieved can be attributed to labour and capital inputs. The remaining half is explained by technological progress. [Similar results were earlier established by Kendrik (1961)]. Of late, Binswanger and Ruttan's (1978) 'theory of induced technical and institutional change' shows that technical change (in the agricultural sector) is endogenous to the development process, that it is the most important factor responsible for explaining (agricultural) productivity differences among countries and time, and that the process of technical change, instead of being guided by the 'invisible hand', has been propelled by public-sector agricultural research institutions. In the light of this evidence, models of economic development should explicitly feature technological progress as an engine of growth. One implication of this is that the focus of models and public policy should not be just on import substitution of goods but also on import substitution in technological knowledge.[12]

Third, as noted above, development economics will also have to do some load shedding in respect of the various non-operational hypotheses that sustain it. This can be achieved partly by doing solid empirical work. Unlike in neo-classical economics, the econometric revolution engineered by Tinbergen, Klein, and Malinvaud should find a central place in development economics.[13] As shown in greater detail in Chapters 4, 5 and 6, an important assumption in this category is that of Pareto-optimality, whose relevance is somewhat questionable when growth and equity issues must be handled together. However, Pareto-optimality does not necessarily do such heavy-duty jobs. Sen (1970a) notes:

> A society or an economy can be optimal in (the Pareto) sense even when some people are rolling in luxury and others are near starvation, as long as the starvers cannot be made better off without cutting into the pleasures of the rich.

Even though such extreme cases do not render the Pareto-optimality criterion entirely irrelevant, development economics should feature more prominently a lexicographic ordering of individual preferences, such that the needs of the least-privileged in that particular society are adequately met in all possible states of the economy. This advice, which comes out quite strongly from Rawls's (1971) influential work, is relevant to developing countries. A logical consequence of the acceptance of such advice is that considerations of equity acquire at least as much significance as the dictates of efficiency. That being the case, the normative capitalistic principle that what is (privately) profitable is (socially) right must be discarded as undesirable for guiding investment decisions in developing countries, where the widespread phenomena of external economies would rule out an exclusive reliance on market-oriented solutions. Furthermore, there should be explicit rules deciding the desirable form of investment to ensure an adequate flow of wage goods and investment goods rather than that of luxury goods. This is an issue on which, according to Robinson (1979), standard economic theory is silent.

As noted in Chapter 5, concern for the least-privileged

44

should logically lead development economists to enquire systematically into the question of how best to inject moral and ethical considerations into the main corpus of development theory. This is because, as Boulding (1966) pointed out, 'no science of any kind can be divorced from ethical considerations'. In developing economies such a task is not only intellectually challenging but also morally obligatory. It will require a lot of soul-searching and intellectual commitment on the part of development economists to do this job satisfactorily. Development economics need not be the high church of positivity that mainstream economics, which was itself born out of a marriage of philosophy and ethics, has pretended to be. Tinbergen (1982) remarks pertinently: 'Socialist policy, if it wants to shape a future human race living in happiness needs a *more profound basis*—either religious or humanist....' The same holds for a non-socialist policy as well.

NOTES

[1]The empirical part of Schultz's thesis, that the surplus labour theory is a 'false doctrine', has also been shown to be rather weak. Sen (1967) points out that the empirical test performed by Schultz to test the strength of the 'surplus labour' hypothesis is based on data relating to Indian agriculture before and after the influenza epidemic of 1918-19.

[2]Lewis also described the mutual-conflict situation between the underdeveloped and developed countries in his Nobel Lecture (1980). However, it should be noted that in Lewis's presentation, the mutual-conflict situation is set out not as an inexorable law of nature but as a result of the slower growth of world trade relative to the growth during the two decades before 1973.

[3]A rigorous answer to these questions requires an explicit description of the new paradigm, in terms of a 'hard core', a 'positive heuristic' and a 'protective belt'. But in economics, much less development economics, such a description may not be feasible.

[4]See Chapter 7 for a discussion of the cases where growth theory can, all the same, be useful for development economics.

[5]See Blaug (1976) for a discussion of this concept.

[6]See also Khan (1975), (1983).

[7]It is this moral and social chaos, which sometimes is given the incorrect name, 'stability', that made Robinson (1979) declare: 'It is not easy to see how the Third World can mount the attack (on mass poverty) while preserving private property in the means of production and respecting the rules of the free-market economy.'

[8]It is this fact that led Marx (1959) to emphasize that social process constituted an 'indivisible whole.' Much later, it also led Boulding (1966) to declare: 'We are dealing in this case (of economic development) with a total social process, and the economic abstractions are simply not sufficient to deal with the problem.'

[9]This is generally true in the theory of *large* games.

[10]There have been significant recent attempts in mathematical economics to replace such an assumption. For instance, see Khan and Sun (1990). But, in general, the state of neo-classical knowledge is as I have indicated.

[11]It is pertinent to quote Leontief (1983):

> To an insightful observer, such as Adam Smith was, the entire national economy appears to be guided and protected by an Invisible Hand. But neither the classical nor the present-day mathematical economists seem to have realized that the effective operation of the automatic price mechanism depends critically on the nature of the nineteenth-century technology. That technology brought an unprecedented rise in total output, but at the same time it maintained and even strengthened the dominant role of human labour in most kinds of productive processes—thus automatically securing for labour a large and, in many instances, a gradually increasing share of total national income.

[12]The optimality of subsidizing the learning process directly, instead of providing protection to the domestic industry, is a well-established result in those cases where 'externalities' result from the presence of a learning factor. See Naqvi (1969).

[13]Some examples of such new hypotheses flowing from an explicit use of a macro-econometric model are given in Naqvi et al. (1983, 1986).

2

The Ideas of Defunct Economists

An issue of great importance to development economists as well as policy-makers relates to the activities of the 'defunct economist', who keeps being reincarnated to satisfy the (excessive) demand for his services.

Keynes (1936) explicitly assigned a prominent role to the defunct economist in the conduct of economic policy.[1] This statement would naturally lead to the question: which ideas of economists—especially the defunct economists—have held sway over the minds of the policy-makers in developing countries? Not unexpectedly, the defunct economist appears to have been the 'lender of the last resort' in the realm of ideas not only to his regular client, the policy-maker, but also to his adversary, the development economist. But in the early stages of economic development, the policy-maker and the development economist made an attempt to give the impression of a happy marriage between themselves. Although thinking themselves immune to the influence of the economists, the policy-makers in these countries did benefit from the ideas of, for example, Rosenstein-Rodan, Harrod, Domar, Lewis, Rostow, Kaldor, Hirschman and Mahalanobis.[2] However, the rift became noticeable when, with the passage of time, the policy-makers began to involve themselves openly with the defunct economists.

This is not a surprise since the defunct economists have captured the heart not only of the 'madman in authority' (as Keynes called him), but also of some living development economists following the rehabilitation of Adam Smith by the neo-classical economists.[3] Further, the success stories of developing countries like Singapore, South Korea, Taiwan, and Hong Kong have been interpreted as positive proof of Adam Smith's reincarnation and return.[4] There is little reason, however, for the development economist to hide his birthmark because the economies of the Far Eastern Four have been noticeably regulated [Sen (1981a)]. This is especially true of South Korea, which has been advertised widely as the paradise of free-traders where Adam Smith has already staged his Second Coming. Unfortunately, there is no evidence of any festivity in South Korea to mark the event.[5]

To answer our question about the ideas of defunct economists, we need to have a detailed look at each of the three actors in the development episode, namely, the policy-maker, the development economist and the defunct economist.

THE POLICY-MAKER

Any description of the development strategy followed during the 1950s and part of the 1960s must include the activities of the makers of development policy in developing countries, in this case the experiences of Pakistan and India. We shall first look at the development strategy and its makers, and then outline the latter-day modifications made in response to the happenings, both real and imaginary, in the developing countries.

The Religion of Growthmanship

The structure of economic policy in India and Pakistan during the decades of the fifties and the sixties, with some important differences, has broadly consisted of the following elements.

In Pakistan, any explicit commitment to socialistic ideology was ruled out; it was greatly emphasized in India. In practice, however, both countries decided to evolve a capitalistic pattern of production and to commit themselves to growthmanship.[6] It is true that as Bhagwati (1984) informs us, there was some talk in India about growth 'not being an objective in itself but a way of making a sustained assault on poverty', but in fact growthmanship, though somewhat infructuous, was followed relentlessly in India. The need for a heavy investment in the capital-goods-producing sectors at the initial stages of planning was emphasized, with a view to maximizing the consumption of such goods over the planning period. The purpose was to accelerate the growth rate to attain self-sustaining growth in the shortest period of time. In sharp contrast, the light industry option was exercised in Pakistan with better results in terms of realized growth rates. In both the countries 'grow first and distribute later, if at all,' appeared to be the refrain of development policy.

As a commitment to growth, the policy-maker allowed the fruits of economic progress to grow in the immediate neighbourhood of the growth poles in the hope that these would become available to all, rich and poor, through some kind of a backward or forward locomotion of the engine of growth. Since industrialization was 'universally' adopted as the engine of growth, a thriving agriculture was inevitably used to support the nascent industrial sector. Then, driven by an all-pervasive export pessimism and the desire to increase the size of the domestic market, import substitution was adopted as the preferred mode of industrialization. In Pakistan, the industrialization process was initiated by import-substituting consumer goods, especially luxury goods, the import of which had to be curtailed partly for balance-of-payments reasons and partly because of the ready domestic availability of raw materials (such as cotton and jute) and a plentiful domestic supply of cheap labour. By contrast, India, following Mahalanobis (1953), initiated the import-substitution process with investment in heavy industries. By turning the rate of the investment in heavy industries into a policy variable, the Indian policy-maker hoped that the growth of the 'down-stream' consumer goods industries, and that of the total output, would eventually be much greater than if the 'light industry first' option were exercised.

Since the economy could not raise itself by its own bootstraps, foreign aid was accepted as a supplement to domestic savings, which were supposed to rise over time.

The 'aid to end aid' rhetoric was freely used, presumably in all sincerity, in both Pakistan and India. Foreign aid was accepted, rather light-heartedly, to finance economic growth with a view to relieving the domestic resource constraint. True, the goal of self-reliance was explicitly spelled out in successive development plans, but in this respect the deeds seldom matched the words. Foreign aid, which started as a tiny trickle, soon assumed the proportions of a vast torrent.

There was also a consensus among the policy-makers that the task of achieving economic growth, balanced or un-balanced, required direct and indirect state intervention. As such, the planned route to development was accepted in both Pakistan and India, which launched their own Five-Year Plans. Public investment (savings) was planned, but private investment (savings) was regulated indirectly by a set of fiscal, monetary, credit, and trade policies. These policies, acting in unison as well as at cross purposes, had the effect of literally providing a captive market to the domestic (private) producers by removing the threat of foreign com-petition as well as the effect of maximizing the investible surplus in the hands of the capitalists with the aim of achieving high rates of private investment and industrial growth.[7]

The Emergence of a New-Old Religion

Through a curious process of learning and unlearning from recent history, policy-makers, especially in Pakistan, were persuaded to agree on a new-old structure of economic policy. The main elements of the policy were:
1. The maximization of growth, but with a substantially larger allocation than was made in the past for such 'basic needs' as clean water, housing, electricity, and education. That this is growthmanship with a larger provision for social services is another matter; the main point of this new-old strategy is to deal directly with the problems

faced by those who live below the 'poverty line', rather than leave them to the trickle-down effects of higher economic growth.[8]

2. Far greater emphasis on agriculture than in the past, though not as the engine of progress. The emphasis of economic policy should be on increasing production, especially agricultural production. Yet structural reforms in the agricultural sector that aim at changing the balance of economic power and promise considerable gains in productive efficiency should be postponed.[9]

3. The active pursuit of export promotion to balance the earlier preoccupation with import substitution, which was shown to have led to allocative inefficiency in the industrial sector. Import-liberalization policy was advocated and actively pursued to cure these inefficiencies. Furthermore, the earlier export pessimism was found not to be entirely justified as export promotion measures did pay off. The extraordinary growth of world trade at about 8 per cent per annum for two full decades until 1973 also helped to erode the earlier export pessimism.

4. The minimization of government intervention in economic activity in order to give market forces a free rein. The private sector should be encouraged, with all the incentives that it takes, to eliminate the wasteful rent-seeking activities due to government activities. This unleashing of the forces of market, it was hoped, would increase efficiency and improve productivity.

The goal of independence of foreign aid and even of foreign loans need not be pursued actively because, as in the past, aid is required to bridge the investment-savings gap. Breaking a time-honoured tradition can be a risky affair, much more so now than in the past. At any rate, more aid is needed to service and pay off old debts as well. Also, considering that official aid comes at only nominal rates of interest, implying negative real interest rates, it is a (nearly) free gift.

THE DEVELOPMENT ECONOMIST

Apart from the policy-maker, the development economist also has had much to do with the course of the strategy adopted. Thus, it is appropriate to ask: To what extent is this course of policy-making traceable to the thinking of the development economist?

The Age of Chivalry

The central idea of the new discipline of development economics was to achieve rapid rates of economic growth. To Harrod (1939, 1970) and Domar (1946, 1957) we owe the apparently simple concept—in fact, a magical formulation—that the warranted rate of growth is exclusively a function of the marginal savings rate and the capital-output ratio. Precisely because the concept looked so manageable, it provided much food for thought to a whole generation of development economists and policy-makers. An acceleration of physical capital formation was seen as the key to economic progress (see Chapter 7). Early on, Rosenstein-Rodan (1943), writing about the experience of the Western countries as developing economies, thought of industrialisation as the principal engine of growth. Then, the many historical studies of the England of 1776, of Communist Russia after 1917, and of Japan during the Meiji period emphasized the supporting role of agriculture in the process of economic development, with the industrial sector cast as the star performer.[10]

Subscribing to these ideas, Lewis (1954) put (physical) capital formation firmly at the centre of the development process. He declares: 'First, it should be noted that our subject-matter is growth, and not distribution.' This statement followed logically from his earlier work (1954) in which he showed that there was no need for reconciliation between growth and equity. Indeed, a necessary condition for promoting economic development is that the share of profits in total national income must rise to generate the capitalist surplus required to finance capital accumulation. He states candidly:

> "We are interested not in the people in general, but only say in the 10 percent of them with the largest income, who in countries with surplus labour receive up to 40 percent of the national income.... Our problem then becomes [sic] what are the circumstances in which the share of profits in national income increases. [11]

Assuming that the demand conditions are the right ones and the industrial sector is essentially self-sufficient in the sense of having no trade with the agricultural sector, the growth of the manufacturing sector—the engine of growth—will be accelerated so long as labour is transferred from the agricultural sector at an unchanged real wage. All profits are assumed to be saved and readily invested. In contrast with Harrod's formulation, in which the saving ratio is constant, Lewis postulated that the key to rapid economic growth is the raising of the saving ratio to a high enough level to finance the required rate of investment through a process of structural transformation. As pointed out by Chenery (1983), the central feature of this structural transformation is the growth-generating reallocation of labour among sectors in the Lewis model, as opposed to the neo-classical growth model in which the sectoral composition of growth is irrelevant.[12] Furthermore, Lewis clearly painted a scenario in which a widening inequality of income between the income groups and between the agricultural and industrial sectors is a necessary condition for rapid economic growth.

Subsequent empirical studies by Kuznets (1955) conferred some respectability on this line of thought by showing that income distribution follows a U-shaped trajectory. It first worsens, then improves, and then worsens again as economic growth proceeds apace. Kaldor (1955) and Galenson and Leibenstein (1955) laid the foundation of a theory that supported the policy of generating investible surplus in the (corporate) manufacturing sector. Kaldor assumes that the wage-earner's marginal propensity to save is nearly zero, and that of the capitalist close to 1, so that growth equilibrium in the Kaldorian sense is determined exclusively by the savings rate of the capitalist. Galenson and Leibenstein advocate the 'critical minimum effort' thesis, which requires that savings be placed in the hands of those who are inclined to save the most—namely, the capitalist.

Hirschman's theory of unbalanced growth (1958) and that of Perroux (1955) lay emphasis on the growth poles from where, through the trickle-down effect, the benefits of growth are assumed to spread throughout the economy (1958). Myrdal also spoke of the spread effects (1956). That these growth poles could enfeeble the periphery of their growth potential was not sufficiently emphasized. Prebisch (1959) advocated the export-pessimism thesis, which justified an 'inward-looking' pattern of development in which import substitution was supposed to take the driver's seat. This prescription, coupled with the general notion that the main constraining factor in the developing countries came from the supply-side, and not from any deficiency of effective demand, was used as a justification for the policy bias of protecting domestic (infant) industries through import licensing and capital-cheapening policies.

In India, the Mahalanobis-Feldman hypothesis, which was formulated within the context of a closed economy and the complete non-shiftability of capital stock from the consumption-goods sector to the investment-goods sector, argued for the setting up a capital-goods base first to achieve high rates of saving, capital formation, and economic growth by imposing suitable constraints on 'initial' consumption. Bhagwati and Chakravarty (1969) inform us that at about the same time in India the alternative Brahmanand-Vakil hypothesis (1956) assigned to the production of wage goods, especially food, the key role in the promotion of economic growth. This was done mainly by mobilizing the disguised unemployed, who were seen as the bearers of substantial (potential) savings. Apparently, this hypothesis was overshadowed by the brilliance of the Mahalanobis model which formed the basis of India's Second Five-Year Plan.

It is explicitly recognized, especially in the balanced-growth scenario sketched by Rosenstein-Rodan (1943) and Nurkse (1953), that the course of economic growth must be consciously guided by the state. On the other hand, Hirschman (1958) thinks that, even without a planned effort, an unbalanced growth strategy will draw into the open—somewhat mysteriously—'hidden' entrepreneurial and other resources, which will respond to the challenges posed by economic growth. However, taking a leaf from Pigou (1924), there was a near-consensus among development economists that, in view of the 'failures' of the market that presumably occur more frequently in the developing than in the developed countries, so important an objective as economic development could not be left entirely to the market.

This is the paradigm that the majority of development economists subscribed to during what I refer to as the age of chivalry. The predominant sentiment among development economists was one of optimism: of slaying the dragon of poverty by the 'simple' manoeuvre of raising the rate of capital accumulation, along a 'balanced' or unbalanced growth path. The industrial sector was the engine of growth, propelled by import-substituting industrialization. As the resource constraint was the only one binding constraint, this objective could only be achieved by a combination of a critical minimum domestic saving effort and foreign aid.[13]

The Age of Enlightenment

It is also important to consider some of the relatively recent ideas of development economists, which could have directly influenced development policy.

Since growth with equity should be the central theme of development economics, attempts have been made to develop growth models that explicitly attach welfare weights to growth indices, and which prescribe that the redistributive effort had better concentrate on the marginal increments in income [14] [Chenery et al. (1974)]. There were also those who advocated a direct attack on poverty because economic growth per se is not very efficient for meeting the basic needs of those living below the poverty line, such as, education, health, electricity, and clean water [Streeten (1980)]. In 1975, the Dag Hammarskjold Foundation pleaded for 'another development' on the conviction that 'resources are available to satisfy basic needs without transgressing the "outer limits".' The next year, the ILO advocated that 'development planning should include as an explicit goal the satisfaction of an absolute level of basic needs'. At about the same time, many scholars of the World Bank research team under Robert McNamara vigorously advocated the basic-needs strategy which assigned a low priority to economic growth per se and focused mainly on the supply of clean water, health, and housing facilities for the bottom 40 per cent (or 30 per cent) of the population as the main indicators of the economic development that really mattered.

Even more fundamental was the assertion, which was not supported by any formal proof, that additional allocation to such social services is unambiguously growth-promoting. The basic needs strategy was also offered as an alternative, rather than as a supplement, to structural change. Streeten et al. (1981) emphasized this point, contraposing egalitarianism and humanism, the latter being identified with the provision of basic needs, as two mutually exclusive objectives. But such an either–or position is not at all basic to the main argument. Indeed, it is artificial and can be maintained only by neglecting the demand blade of the Marshallian scissors. The supply of basic needs, Streeten's humanism, must be matched by an increase in the real income of the poorer sections of the society, both in absolute terms and relative to that of the rich, in order to claim egalitarianism.

Chakravarty (1984) argued that the exclusion of effective demand as a factor constraining growth from the development paradigm might have been a little too hasty. Furthermore, Mellor and Johnston (1984) showed that the growth-promoting potentialities of a deliberate policy of raising the real income of the rural poor must be recognized, by keeping the price of food low for this income group whose propensity to spend on food is in the 0.5–0.9 range. This can be done through a rationing system, or by taxing the marketed agricultural surplus, or both. Such a policy would keep within reasonable limits the food-feed competition which tends to lower the availability of food to the urban and rural poor [Yotopoulos (1985)]. As long as the wage rate in the industrial sector is higher than in the agricultural sector, and the price of capital services remains positive and high, the demand-propelled forces of growth emanating from the agricultural sector may help to promote a dynamic balance between the industrial and agricultural sectors—a balanced-growth scenario in which the forces of both the supply-side and the demand-side play a significant role.

It follows from this line of reasoning that the concept of the sole engine of growth should be discarded, as it creates problems by way of introducing intersectoral disequilibria.[15] The development process is best seen as an integrated one and not one following an 'unbalanced' trajectory, for the simple reason that the market, left to itself, tends to concentrate rather than diffuse the benefits of growth. Agriculture and industry must grow together, instead of one financing the other. Ruttan (1982) made this point explicitly by bringing in appropriate technological change as a factor ensuring sectoral balance and economic growth.

The need for achieving a balance between export promotion and import substitution was emphasized in the empirical work on trade policy. The underlying themes were that the export-pessimism thesis, propounded by earlier economists like Prebisch, should not be taken too literally by developing countries, that conscious programmes of export expansion and import liberalization offer real possibilities of efficient growth, and that, in so far as export industries tend to be relatively labour-intensive, such a policy shift should also help income distribution, if only to a limited extent.

The rate of growth, as also the composition and quality of growth, is a function not only of physical capital but also of human capital. According to this line of thought, first formulated in 1962 by Schultz (1962) and Becker (1962), such diverse activities as education, health, job search, migration, and in-service training, are rational acts of investment in human capital which link present decisions to future returns. A related idea, much emphasized in a large number of studies pioneered by Solow (1957) and Denison (1962), is that, historically, the most important determinant of growth has been technological progress, which again is a function of the level of educational attainment in the society. (See Chapter 7.)

There is also the problem of effecting structural change, and not merely of accelerating the growth of output, as a means of raising the economic well-being of the poor.[16] In this context, the question of an egalitarian redistribution of assets, in particular of land holdings, holds the key to an orderly growth process which also contributes to resolving the problem of poverty.[17] By contrast, Sen (1981) sets out a theory of 'entitlement' which, he pleads, should become the focal point of a new paradigm of economics. A person's entitlement consists of his 'ownership' and his exchange possibilities, which together determine his overall endowment.[18] (See Chapter 5 for details.)

THE DEFUNCT ECONOMIST

A comparison of the teachings of development economists and the (mal)practices of policy-makers clearly points to increasingly deviant behaviour by the latter with the passage of time. While earlier, the ideas of development economists were somewhat faithfully reflected in the Five-Year Plans, this happy equation changed with the passage of time, for instance, the emphasis on the equity objective is no more than mere lip-service. The attempts at structural change to redesign the structure of property rights and the recognition of the role of human capital are no better than in the past. In short, while the policy-maker understood the development economist as long as he talked about economic growth, there has been a clear lack of communication about the process of economic development. This brings us to that mysterious character, the defunct economist, who, according to Keynes, is a permanent mentor of the 'madmen in authority', that is, the policy-makers, and whose appointed role is to upset the apple-cart of the living idea-givers. Who is this notorious defunct economist, and what explains his pervasive influence on policy-makers, especially in the developing countries?

The problem of identifying a defunct economist has all the markings of the well-known identification problem in econometrics. For instance, how do you distinguish a defunct economist from a living economist, in the midst of the scatter of observations which seem to indicate both types simultaneously?

A promising approach to the problem is to recognize a defunct economist as one who is the active practitioner of what Lakatos (1970) calls a 'degenerating' Scientific Research Programme (SRP), as opposed to a 'progressive' SRP, whose practitioners are the living economists. (See Chapter 1). Hicks (1976) offers a philosophical-cum-historical explanation of this identification problem which should be especially to the liking of the policy-maker. He opines that, unlike a natural scientist for whom the 'old ideas are worked out [and] old controversies are dead and buried', an economist cannot throw overboard the dead weight of the past. That explains why '"neo-classical" succeeds neo-mercantilist; Keynes and his contemporaries echo Ricardo and Malthus; Marx and Marshall are still alive'. That may well be so, but, in my opinion, in economics like in other sciences, old ideas do get worked out with the passage of time, making way for new, and more relevant ones.[19] There have been genuine 'revolutions' in the realm of economics in the sense that a 'progressive' SRP, with excess empirical content, replaces a 'degenerating' SRP, even though not necessarily in the Kuhnian (1962) sense of a 'discontinuous jump' from one ruling 'paradigm' to another with no conceptual bridge between the two. Thus, defunct economists should be distinguished from the living economists, even though the former may also be doing the part-time job of ensuring a continuity of ideas.

Having proven the 'existence' of the defunct economist, we are now in a position to consider a more practical question: Why do policy-makers open their hearts to the defunct economist but turn frigid at the sight of a living economist? Do we have here a case of Gresham's Law in which the defunct drive the living out of circulation? Lewis offers a somewhat offhand answer to such questions. He thinks that most problems, in both the developed and the developing economies, seem to be amenable to the time-honoured tools of economics, viz., Supply and Demand and the Quantity Theory of Money

—and, one may add, the Say's Law. 'This is why,' Lewis (1984) asserts, 'there are so many good untrained economists, and also why some of our most high-powered colleagues perform no better than a good undergraduate'. If the intellectual endowment of many developing countries consists of little besides the talents of good (or bad) undergraduates, the views of the defunct economist on economic matters should enjoy an exalted status in developing countries. Whether this is the actual state of affairs is another matter.

The fact is that development economists, and not only neo-classical economists, have for long distilled their wisdom from Adam Smith and Ricardo. Lewis openly pleads that development economists should keep in close contact with the work of Adam Smith. This explains the supply-side bias in the thinking of the (practising) development economists, who have, all along, emphasized the central position of capital accumulation in the growth process. Also, the development literature highlights the mystical propensities of capitalists to invest their profits, and even rents, in what is good for society. That no empirical study of stature has confirmed such a Cal-vinist altruism on the part of the modern capitalist has not made certain development economists doubt the efficacy of their stock recipes for the benefit of developing countries. Besides, in his search for a suitable formula for growth, the development economist, according to Lewis, has consulted nearly all his ancestors, from the remote and recent past, namely:

the physiocrats for agriculture; the mercantilists for export surplus; the classicists for free market; the Marxists for capital; the neoclassicists for entrepreneurship; the Fabians for government; the Stalinists for [heavy] industrialization; the Chicago School for schooling; and econometricians like E.F. Denison for a large residual.

As if to prove the strength of his Pavlovian reflex, the development economist has continued to consult these predecessors, even though not one of these earlier 'drivers' ever succeeded in driving single-handedly and at full steam the (now worn-out) engine of growth. Furthermore, the defunct economist appears to be gaining new ground with the emergence of a neoclassical political economy, according to which the Invisible Hand is not allowed to work by the so-called 'Invisible Foot' —that is, the forces that prevent competition from working for the larger good of society [Collandar (1984)]. While the work on the rent-seeking phenomenon and directly-unproductive profit-seeking (DUP) activities by Krueger, Bhagwati and Srinivasan is most valuable in pointing out how state intervention should not be conducted, it does not necessarily prove that state intervention should be eliminated altogether and that things should instead be entrusted to the Invisible Hand.[20] Between the opposing poles of the market and the government lies a whole territory where these characters can, and should, meet in friendly embrace. (See Chapter 6.)

FACING THE CHALLENGE

Blaug (1983) has noted that major economic doctrines are not only a scientific research programme (SRP) but also a political action programme (PAP). 'It is only when a theory defines both a "progressive" SRP and "progressive" PAP that we can talk of a revolution in economic thought; (the obvious example is Keynesian economics in the 1930s).' In light of the discussion above, it should be clear that development economics is both an SRP and a PAP. To make it truly 'progressive', its empirical content and relevance for fruitful policy action will have to be enhanced. For all the heroic effort made to establish their distinctive identity, the practitioners of development economics will have to do a lot of homework in order to make their presence felt in the realm of policy-making. As things are, there appears to be a fundamental incongruity in the realm of ideas as well as between the ideas and the reality. What needs to be done, as Keynes did in the wake of the Great Depression, is to make development economics reflect the economic, political, social and ethical realities of the developing countries. A return to the fold of neo-classical economics would definitely be a move in the wrong direction. This does not mean that neo-classical economics is irrelevant, but that the deep insights it offers into the economic phenomenon needs to be re-focused and combined with additional ones to deal with the problematic of the development process.

The things the development economist must eschew for good are an exclusive reliance either on promoting high growth rates or on ensuring distributive justice, a hasty and irreversible retreat to the cold embrace of an unpredictable market, an implicit belief in the existence and stability of the capitalist's 'conscience' [Gilder (1981)], along with an insufficient understanding of the structural difficulties in transforming saving into a socially optimal form of investment, an ever-increasing dependence on foreign aid, a persistent refusal to recognize the importance of technological change and human capital formation, especially of education, in the process of economic growth, and a non-comprehension of the role of structural change in the process of economic development. In particular, it is one thing to recognize the importance of the market as an information gatherer, but it is quite another (and a wrong) thing to unquestioningly accept such information to be final. Tinbergen (1977) has argued that the challenge facing the economist is to turn, through a process of trial and error, government's economic policy into a 'coherent entity' in such a manner that economic growth is linked firmly to the process of income distribution. This exercise will require, among other things, that there be as many policy instruments as there are policy objectives and that there be not only an investment plan but also a plan regarding the process of income generation. Such a decision, however, will require a kind of intellectual activism that does not follow blindly the automatic laws of economics to take care of the affairs of the real world.[21]

Once the development economist has settled his score with the defunct economist, the economic visibility of the development policy-maker will grow immeasurably. It should then be clear that the main task of the policy-maker in developing countries is to create socio-economic and political institutions that also facilitate structural change. Development economics, even at the risk of offending Lionel Robbins, must reflect the social and political realities of the developing world. Its practitioners must show a greater understanding of the realities in the developing countries, as it would help them to create new knowledge.[22] In particular, the real income of the rural poor must increase, both directly and indirectly, to ensure a balanced growth of agriculture and industry and to establish a link between income distribution, economic growth, and employment.

NOTES

[1]Indeed, if the iconoclast of the *General Theory* were a development economist he would have exorcised the ghost of the defunct economist from its realm, even if that meant setting up a few stuffed shirts to be shot down. No worshipper at the temples of Adam Smith and David Ricardo, Keynes did not believe in the unlimited magic of the market or in the institution of (unlimited) private property.

[2]However, it may be noted that, contrary to Keynesian intentions, some of these development economists themselves drew inspiration from defunct economists like Adam Smith and David Ricardo.

[3]The neo-classical economists have finally secured Adam Smith's message for posterity by proving the Fundamental Theorem of Welfare Economics: 'Every competitive equilibrium is a Pareto-optimum; and, if initial endowments are suitably redistributed through lumpsum transfers, every Pareto-optimum is a competitive equilibrium.' [For a careful statement of the theorem see Khan (1987b)].

[4]While this Gang of Four has achieved great success by any standards, one important contributory factor must have been that, for strategic reasons, their defence needs were fully met by the United States.

[5]Sen (1983) has argued, 'if this is a free market [in South Korea] then Walras's auctioneers can surely be seen as going around with a government white paper in one hand and a whip in another.'

[6]For a detailed account of the government-sponsored private capitalism in Pakistan, see Papanek (1967), and Lewis (1969).

[7]For a brief history of Pakistan's experience in the fifties and the mid-sixties, see Naqvi (1982). A good account of Pakistan's first two Five-Year Plans is given in Haq (1963). Bhagwati and Chakravarty (1969) provide a comprehensive analysis of India's first three Five-Year Plans.

[8]Inspired by the Sri Lankan experience, such a line of thought has been advanced by many economists. See, for example, Sen (1983).

[9]For an interesting account of the effect of structural reforms and other factors on Pakistan's agriculture, see Khan (1983), while some special aspects of Indian agriculture are analysed in Krishna (1963).

[10]For an excellent study of the Japanese example of agriculture as a sustainer of industrial development and for the relevance of this example for developing countries, see Okhawa et al. (1970) especially Chapter 3.

[11]It is interesting to recall here that the 'bloody-mindedness' about economic growth and the lack of concern for income (and wealth) distribution displayed by Lewis (1954) and some others like Galenson and Leibenstein (1955) in the fifties and even earlier by Schumpeter (1934), parallels the sentiment of Adam Smith in 1776 when he set out to explore only 'the nature and cause of the wealth of nations'. He was followed by David Ricardo who was only secondarily concerned with distribution. It was left for (Stuart) Mill to emphasize the primary importance of distribution in the scheme of things that political economy should be concerned about. The stage was thus set for Marxian distributive socialism, which equated capitalist surplus with capitalistic exploitation. True, the leaders of the 'marginalist revolution' did try to explain away the capitalist-exploitation by reference to the imaginary episode of each factor of production

receiving its just reward, but according to Robinson (1979), this defence, based on a confusion between the sources of income and the factors of production, was by and large ineffectual, generating neither heat nor light.

[12]As pointed out by Chenery (1983), the central feature of this structural transformation is the growth-generating reallocation of labour among sectors in the Lewis model as opposed to the neo-classical growth model in which the sectoral composition of growth is irrelevant.

[13]The question as to whether aid helped or hindered economic growth in the developing countries has spawned a vast literature. For the typical agnostic view, see Griffin and Enos (1970), while Papanek (1972) has been in the vanguard of the defenders of the faith. He has shown that the agnostics' case, that foreign aid tends to supplant domestic saving instead of supplementing it, was mistakenly based on the assumption that saving equals investment minus foreign-aid inflows, from which it followed that 'as long as the effect of an additional unit of foreign resources on investment is less than one, its effect on savings will appear to be negative.'

[14]See, Naqvi and Qadir (1985).

[15]Lewis (1984) observes that 'given the range of possibilities, the search for "the" engine of growth must be foredoomed'.

[16]Reynolds (1977) has appropriately pointed out that 'the core of the subject [of development economics] is longitudinal analysis of growth and structural change in... economies that have entered the phase of growth acceleration' (p.12).

[17]The central importance of a 'radical structural change' for achieving 'equitable economic growth' has been brought out in sharp relief in the work of Adelman and Morris (1973).

[18]Sen (1983) writes: 'Given the functional relation between entitlements of persons over goods and their capabilities a useful—though derivative— characterization of economic development is in terms of the expansion of entitlements.' He has also emphasized that such an expansion of entitlements will require active State intervention.

[19]Reynolds (1977) also shows excessive reverence to the classical writers and pleads that they be not considered 'relics of a bygone era'. We may accept his plea and yet disagree, for reasons given in the text, with his judgement that 'the classical economists wrestled with problems that confront economists in India, Nigeria, or Brazil' (p. 20). Be that as it may, it certainly does not follow from Reynolds's judgement that development economists should hold exactly the same theories and views as held by the classical economics more than two hundred years ago.

[20]An interesting example of the contention made in the text is provided in a study of wheat markets in Pakistan by Naqvi and Cornelisse (1986) which shows that the policy of procurement of wheat by the government,

Development Economics

while quite defectively implemented, is still required to prevent the private traders in the wheat market from becoming exploitative. And this despite the fact that the private traders' marketing margins are quite low! [21]Samuelson (1966) remarks:

> how treacherous are economic 'laws' in economic life: e.g. Bowley's Law of constant relative wage share; Long's Law of constant population participation in the labour force; Pareto's Law of unchangeable inequality of incomes; Denison's Law of constant private saving ratio; Colin Clark's Law of a 25 per cent ceiling on government expenditure and taxation; Modigliani's Law of constant wealth-income ratio; Marx's Law of the falling rate of real wage and/or the falling rate of profit; Everybody's Law of a constant capital-output ratio. If these be laws, Mother Nature is a criminal by nature (p. 1539).

[22]As shown by Sen (1981), once it comes to ensuring a person's entitlement to food, 'it becomes a matter of political and social pressures', which force us to break through the narrow confines of economics—especially development economics. Bhagwati (1984) provides another interesting example of such knowledge creation: 'It is hard, for instance, for development economists to consider now the role of multinationals in development without considering the possibility that the optimal mix of tax-cum-subsidy policies on trade and capital flows... may simply be infeasible...' These are only two examples of the creative role that awaits the policy-makers.

3

The Visible Hand and
the Invisible Hand

Of late, the role of the 'government' has become the central issue both in the academic ivory towers and in the corridors of power. Liberal opinion has drawn strength and gained support after the recent events in Eastern Europe and the disintegration of the Soviet Union. We may now take a closer look at the role of government in the development process, a matter alluded to briefly in the preceding pages. We will see in this chapter that the middle-of-the-road philosophy of economic development, advocating a judicious mix of the market and the government, the proportion of which, however, cannot be decided in advance, is founded in sound economics. By the same token, the liberals' assertion about a generalized market failure is essentially wrongheaded. The mixed-economy route to development is preferable because, while free markets by themselves may lead to a Pareto-optimal constellation of production and consumption (that is, a state in which not everyone's welfare can be increased simultaneously, so that if someone is to gain, others must lose), such an optimum is not necessarily unique. There may be many such optima, depending on the desired distribution of income. Hence, as the Fundamental Theorem of Welfare Economics insists, free markets can maximize social welfare only if supplemented with the appropriate mechanism to regulate the distribution of income and wealth. By themselves, free markets cannot yield optimal social choice globally, especially in the cases in which choices among alternative courses of action have to be made under conditions of uncertainty. Such a possibility is illustrated well by the parable concerning the Prisoner's Dilemma, which is a situation in which both the prisoners ('rational' utility-maximizers) get the worst of all the possible worlds because they opted to act selfishly rather than in concert. (For a fuller development of this argument, see Chapter 6.)

THE MAKING AND UNMAKING OF A MIXED ECONOMY CONSENSUS

Evolution of a Consensus

As I noted in the previous chapter, a near-consensus evolved during the 1950s and 1960s around a philosophy of economic development that incorporated the basic features of the Harrod-Domar growth theory and the Keynesian theory. While economic development is assumed to be a function of (physical) capital formation, the problem of inadequate effective demand is also recognized, though not always adequately emphasized. The central theme of the philosophy is 'balanced growth', made prominent by Nurkse (1953), but first spelled out in Rosenstein-Rodan's (1943) 'big push' conjecture. While these hypotheses envisage only the balanced growth of various components of the industrial sector—'a wave of capital investments in a number of different industries', the basic message is that the key sectors of the economy should grow harmoniously to make full use of the inter-sectoral feedbacks for the purpose of accelerating economic growth. Lewis's dual-economy model sets up a mechanism to achieve a dynamic balance between key sectors of the economy by a reallocation of labour from the agricultural sector to the industrial sector. This is because the marginal productivity of labour is assumed to be higher in the former sector than in the latter. This process continues as long as the wage rate in the industrial sector is higher than in the agricultural sector and the price of capital services in the former remains both high and positive. One of the most fruitful generalizations of the hypothesis put forward by Rosenstein-Rodan and Nurkse is suggested by Chenery (1965). According to him, the key problem is that of 'balancing supply and demand for different commodities and factors of production'. This approach, using input-output analysis, provides a check on the consistency and feasibility of specific development plans. It also allows computation of shadow prices associated with the given investment programmes and, utilizing them, permits an explicit analysis of the possibilities of improving a given investment.

The basic point in the present context is that a balanced growth of various components of the industrial sector or of different sectors of the economy cannot possibly be brought about by free markets alone. Nurkse explicitly stated: 'Economic progress is not a spontaneous or automatic affair. On the contrary, it is evident that there are automatic forces within the system tending to keep it moored to a given level'. Rosenstein-Rodan (1984) is equally candid on this point:

> The programming of investment in a developing country is necessary to correct for such distortions as indivisibilities, externalities, and information failures. 'Programming' is just another word for rational, deliberate, consistent, and coordinated economic policy.

Hence the need for taking a planned route to development. However, this prognosis was never confused with the centrally planned route to development which communist countries advocated and practised. Indeed, such an option was explicitly rejected by developlment economists quite early in the debate.

Subsequent writings of development economists have emphasized an essentially corrective role of the government in managing the process of economic development. Prebisch (1984) clearly envisaged 'an active role' for the state in development planning, which was needed to induce 'structural change' and to 'intensify the rate of internal capital formation'. Mahalanobis's model for India (1953) envisaged a policy-induced—indeed, policy-pushed—development of heavy industries to accelerate capital formation and economic growth. Of late, Mellor (1986) and many other writers have noted, in respect of promoting a balanced sectoral growth, that it is essential to pursue a deliberate policy of raising the real income of the rural poor by keeping the price of food lower than would prevail in the free market. A similar line of reasoning appeared in a World Bank study (1986). Economists who subscribe to this school of thought openly advocate an activist role for the government without de-emphasizing the informational and allocative economies that free markets achieve at a minimal cost. That policy-makers have dutifully accepted this advice is evident from the large number of medium-term (indicative) plans that have guided the public-sector development efforts in developing countries.

The Dissenters: There have been dissenting voices against the reigning development paradigm from its very inception. Indeed, among its founding fathers, Hirschman calls himself a 'second generation dissenter'.[1] He describes himself as fighting a 'major battle in his *strategy* against the widely alleged need for a "balanced" or "big push" industrialization effort' (1984). Accordingly, his 'unbalanced growth' hypothesis is a search for 'hidden rationalities' in the 'processes of growth and change already under way'. With the help of backward and forward linkages, unbalanced growth would somehow enlist latent entrepreneurial talent to energize an otherwise dormant economy. Clearly, Hirschman did not prescribe that sectoral imbalances should be deliberately engineered. Galenson and Leibenstein's (1955) advocacy of their 'critical minimum effort thesis' put the capitalist at the centre of the development process. They and, subsequently, Kaldor (1955) asserted that since a wage-earner's marginal propensity to save was nearly zero, and that of a capitalist close to unity, the growth equilibrium would be determined exclusively by the savings rate of the capitalist.

But the dissenters never went so far as to discount the role of government in economic management completely. Hirschman remains skeptical about the efficiency of the free market. His idea of a 'strategy' implies an effort by the government to call forth and enlist 'development resources and abilities that are hidden, scattered, or badly utilized' (1953). What he was fighting against was the 'myth of Integrated Investment Planning'. Also, in the Galenson-Leibenstein scenario, the state is supposed to support the capitalist through fiscal and monetary policies, and to guide him through specific investment techniques and criteria. Thus, the prevalent consensus in favour of the government was never seriously questioned, although the dissenters did not confirm it either.

The Loyal Opposition: In the first group of development economists are included mostly advocates of the so-called 'neo-classical political economy'. For economists like Bhagwati and Srinivasan (1982) and Krueger (1974), the problem is to choose an optimal 'form' of government intervention according to the merits of the case. When it is shown that quantitative trade restrictions give rise to a lot of activities of the unproductive 'rent-seeking' type, or of the 'directly unproductive profit-seeking' (DUP) type, an important implication is that such restrictions ought to be replaced by tariff restrictions and, when the distortions in question are domestic in nature, the tariffs need to be replaced by export subsidies or by optimal tax-cum-subsidy policies. The effect of many of these suggested 'reforms' is to lower the overall incidence of government intervention, but not to oppose government intervention per se. Too often, however, members of this new 'school' somewhat come close to making out a case for a generalized market success rather than one of selective market failure. (See Chapter 6.)

The Rebels: Among the dissenters are also those who are opposed to all government intervention on the ground that the fact of 'market failure' does not mean that government will not fail in similar circumstances. One of the earliest dissenters is Bauer (1972). He remains to this day a model agnostic in adopting an extremist posture on the issue. Indeed, he accepts *nothing* that development economists say or do. To quote a recent summing up that he has done of his own work: 'I noted then that comprehensive central planning was certainly not necessary for economic advance; it was much more likely to retard it'. Instead, he remains convinced that, just as in the plantation economies of the then British West Africa that he visited and wrote about in the 1930s, economic development had occurred—and, if not, then it would certainly occur—owing to 'the individual voluntary responses of millions of people to emerging or expanding opportunities created largely by external contacts and brought to their notice in a variety of ways, primarily through the operation of the market' (1984).

Then, there are those among development economists who, in their proselytizing zeal, condemn all forms of government intervention as sinful. For instance, Lal (1983) blames 'the *dirigiste* dogma for the most serious current distortions in many developing countries', and explicitly rules out the possibility of steering 'a middle course between *laissez faire* and the *dirigiste* dogma'. As such, he emphasizes that developing countries will be better off in the company of free markets than in the protective custody of the government. According to him, even the theoretically justifiable 'forms' of government intervention are harmful because they tend to work perversely in practice. Hence, a one-way journey from government control to free markets, with no provision for a stop-over at some intermediate station, is the only way to achieve both economic growth *and* equity for the simple reason that government intervention itself is responsible for the less than complete realization of these policy objectives. The implication is that the market always succeeds, even in cases where its failure has been duly acknowledged—for instance, in the case of public goods and externalities of various kinds.

But where do these dissenters draw their inspiration from? To answer this question, let us have a look at the development economist's backyard.

HAPPENINGS IN THE DEVELOPMENT ECONOMIST'S BACKYARD

The Dissolution of the Neo-Keynesian Consensus

Bell and Kristol (1981) suggest, though not entirely convincingly, that the 'house that Keynes built' is in disarray, and that the neo-Keynesian synthesis, elaborately forged by Hicks, Samuelson, Tobin, Modigliani and many others in order to reconcile Keynesian macroeconomics with the classical microeconomics is about to disintegrate. Therefore, it will be relevant here to try to perceive the connection between the reported sense of crisis in neo-Keynesian economics and the prevailing identity crisis among development economists.

The conflict between the monetarists and those who call themselves 'rational expectationists' (or 'ratex'), on the one hand, and the neo-Keynesians, on the other, revolves round the appropriateness of government intervention in the conduct of economic policy. Klamer (1984) notes that the basic question being addressed by the two adversaries is: 'Can the government help to stabilize the economy through active, interventionist policies?' Modigliani (1977) states that while the neo-Keynesians advocate an active interventionist policy for stabilizing the economy through fiscal and monetary policies, the monetarists and rational expectationists say the opposite. According to this latter group, there is no need to stabilize the economy and such attempts are more likely to increase instability than decrease it.

The Neo-Keynesians: The neo-Keynesians are unambiguously persuaded that a 'mixed economy', which is the common characteristic of all the countries outside the former communist bloc, requires redirection and control by the government. Tobin [Klamer (1984), p.10], neatly summarizing the neo-Keynesian position, says: 'I think the basic issue there is the question of whether there are any dead-weight losses or market failures of a macroeconomic nature in a market economy. Neo-Keynesians think that there are, and that the government can do something about them'. Associated with this vision of a 'mixed economy', which, according to the neo-Keynesians is not inherently self-equilibrating, is a deep concern about promoting a socially desirable income distribution that the free market, if left to its devices, cannot take cognizance of. Hence, according to Tobin, 'a neo-Keynesian seems to be more concerned about employment, jobs, and producing goods than people who have great faith in market processes'. These social and political considerations provide an independent justification for government intervention in capitalistic mixed economies where income and wealth are, as a rule, unequally distributed. Fundamentally, the neo-Keynesians hold a relativistic view of human freedom, which must be constrained significantly to maximize social welfare.[2]

The Monetarists: In sharp contrast, the monetarists reject such a world-view. According to Friedman (1968) the economy is inherently self-equilibrating and self-regulating. He maintains that the apparently rigid wages are really not rigid, with the result that the Keynesian involuntary unemployment is not possible. Instead, the Hicksian mechanism, powered by the 'required' changes in the real money supply, ensures full employment. Friedman views a competitive economy, 'disturbed' by a government-induced demand stimulus, as adjusting itself to a 'natural' rate of unemployment *entirely* by the voluntary actions of wage-earners and producers. In his competitive wonderland, wage-earners initially do not 'see' the inflation-induced fall in their real wages, but producers do get a higher price for their produce and 'see' higher profits coming. Thus, unemployment is reduced in the short run. But that is only a temporary phase which, being essentially an optical illusion, is undone by the *voluntary* actions of wage-earners who reduce the additional supply of their services at a lower real wage and contract for higher wages. To make matters worse, inflation rises even as the 'over-heated' economy settles down to the 'natural unemployment-rate'.

The Rational-Expectationists: It should be noted that in Friedman's 'adaptive expectations' model, there is still room for the government to operate effectively along a short-run, negatively sloped Phillips Curve. But according to Lucas (1972) [also Lucas and Sargent (1978)] the government will not succeed in manipulating the economy to its advantage even in the short run.[3] Friedman's adaptive expectations are, in these models, replaced by 'rational expectations', which, in effect, seek to banish Keynesian 'animal spirits' from the world of expectations once and for all. If, instead, the mechanism through which economic agents form expectations are saddled with a rational structure, 'revolutionary' results will follow.

The anarchist message of the rational-expectationists is essentially a call for macro-economic non-management! This is because the economic agents, in reacting to government action, use up all the information that the government has access to. Thus, if the government decides to increase money supply on the basis of some information, the individuals know in advance and alter their behaviour accordingly. Adjustment, therefore, occurs (almost) instantaneously and there is no room for the government, even in the short run, to alter the course of events. Individuals can randomly make mistakes, and it is only in such moments of transient informational lacuna that, according to the so-called Sargent-Wallace proposition (1975), (unanticipated) monetary shocks can produce any tangible effects whatsoever on real macro-economic magnitudes.

As if to make sure that the successive errors of expectations are not serially correlated significantly, the smart actors in the rational-expectations models learn very quickly. They cannot be systematically fooled by the government about its intentions, and can take the economy, all by themselves, to a long-run equilibrium about which they form accurate estimates. Thus, systematic, anticipated monetary or fiscal policies will have no effect on output or employment. Government intervention, according to Lucas, is irrelevant because 'this (U.S.) economy is going to grow at 3 percent a year, no

matter what happens. Forever'.[4] Here, at last, we have a vision
of economic processes that is the closest possible approximation to the physicist's vision of an 'autonomous' universe. In
conformity with the First Law of Motion, according to which
physical bodies keep moving in the same direction and at the
same velocity until something stops them, the economy is
seen by the 'ratex' group as driven by some mysterious
economic laws of motion unless that 'something' called
government stops it.

We may note that in this Galilean vision of real-world
economies, no ethical issues arise from the fact that unemployment prevails because it results from the voluntary actions of
wage-earners themselves. There can also be no social injustice in such a self-equilibrating economy for the simple reason
that government itself is the source of all injustice. Hence,
Lucas discounts any role for the government to resolve social
injustice: 'I can't think of explaining the pharaohs as being in
existence to resolve social injustice in Egypt. I think they
perpetrated most of the injustice in Egypt'[Klamer (1984)].

Thurow (1983) examines in detail the policy nihilism of the
monetarists and the rational-expectationists. First, rational-
expectationists would not allow any possibility of improving
the economic performance by government intervention,
except by mistake. For if there were any such opportunities,
economic agents in Lucas's model would already have acted
upon them and eliminated them. Second, the policy nihilism
of the rational-expectationists, if carried to its logical end,
would immobilize policy-makers for ever. This is because if
economic agents knew everything that government knows and
does, not only would government intervention be unfruitful,
but all attempts to end government intervention would be
equally unfruitful—and for the same reason. Hence, by.virtue
of the omniscience of Lucas's economic agents, the government's decision *not* to intervene would also be counter-productive, even though the decision to intervene was unfruitful

in the first place. Hence, as Thurow observes, 'policy-makers should continue to make the decisions that they were making as if the rational-expectationist hypothesis were not true'. Thus, the Visible Hand, if it exists already, can, by the sheer logic of the rational-expectationist's reasoning, continue to exist for ever!

Modigliani (1977) also rejects the nihilistic message of the rational expectationists: 'We must, therefore, categorically reject the monetarist appeal to turn back the clock forty years by discarding the basic message of the *General Theory*. We should instead concentrate our efforts on an endeavour to make stabilization policies even more effective in the future than they have been in the past'. There are many others, like Tobin, Samuelson and Solow, who express similar sentiments. While acknowledging the great beauty of Adam Smith's creation, Samuelson (1976) would 'not go to the other extreme and become enamoured of the beauty of a pricing mechanism, regarding it as a perfection in itself, the essence of providential harmony, and beyond the touch of human hands.'

From the very beginning of the discipline of development economics, it has been clearly recognized both by its founding fathers and by their successors that there is a place under the sun for both the Visible Hand and the Invisible Hand to work for the good of society. The 'accommodating' attitude of development economists has been broadly consistent with, though not identical to, the neo-Keynesian prescription that, *as long as aggregate demand is kept at the desired level,* free markets can be relied upon to function efficiently. Even though macro stabilization policies do not always figure very prominently in the strategy of planned development, the latter's emphasis on the government's role is very neo-Keynesian. Unlike the communist countries, the developing countries have never questioned the efficacy of the market mechanism as an information-gatherer; it is only that such information is not unquestioningly accepted as a sufficient basis of the actual conduct of public policy. This is because free markets operate not in a vacuum but within a wider institutional framework. Also, there are many important cases of 'external economies'—those not captured by market prices—that vitiate the argument that government has no right to interfere with the working of the free market. However, a complete regimentation of the economy has also not been recommended by any responsible development economist.

As that is the happy middle-of-the-road philosophy that most development economists recommended and policy-makers accepted by common consent, why should anyone try to disturb such (near) consensus among development economists about the relative, and beneficial, roles of the government and the market? If, by calling government inter-vention counter-productive, it is meant that developing countries have fallen behind economically rather than gone forward, then this claim is patently false. Indeed, as Bhagwati (1985) reports, there is nothing in the three decades of development experience to suggest 'increasing immiseriza-tion or even stagnation in the living standards of the poor'. In fact, a look at the successive World Bank Development Reports would show that the rates of growth of per capita income in many developing countries have been quite res-pectable by 'historical' standards, and that the intensity of poverty has been alleviated to varying degrees wherever economic growth has occurred. For instance, the actual per capita growth rates achieved by Pakistan and India would have appeared like a fantasy at the time of their independence from colonial rule. Clark (1984) reports that in 1947 there was a consensus among economists that the Indian economy would at best achieve a long-run growth rate of 0.5 per cent. Pakis-tan's growth possibilities were considered to be much worse.

True, as Meier (1984) points out, there have been 'disap-pointments' experienced by some developing economies.

High rates of population growth, a fairly high level of absolute poverty, and visibly large differences in income and wealth continue to darken the face of the societies in many developing countries. But solving these problems requires an extension of the problem canvas of development economics, and an appropriate policy response. It does not warrant blaming all failures on the government. By the same token, it is not at all helpful to declare the free market as a panacea for all or even most development problems—including those involving structural change.

RAINBOW'S END

If the case for the free market or even, significantly, for free markets, cannot be substantiated empirically, historically, or even theoretically, then why should it be put forward? The rational-expectationist's thesis, that government thrives only on the occasional lapses in the economic agents' informational faculties, is not universally accepted as a sufficient argument for ending the economic role of the government even in the developed countries. There is much less reason for its being accepted in the developing countries, where 'market failures' are a rule rather than an exception, and where the problems of structural change require active government 'intervention'. Arrow (1974) has clearly stated that the 'informational economy' achieved by the market system is not realized when no market exists at all to supply this information in the form of prices. The problem of the non-existence of markets, referred to in the literature as 'market failure', is especially acute with respect to 'future goods'. All such cases, all too common in the developing countries, warrant 'government intervention; code of professional ethics; or of economic organization with some power intermediate between the competitive firm and the government.' Thus, even if, as

The Visible Hand and the Invisible Hand

Becker (1983) warns, governments are nothing but proxies for the vested interests whose interests they serve, this is an argument for having governments which are better and more enlightened, not an excuse for throwing them out altogether.

At a deeper philosophical level, the degree of freedom enjoyed by economic agents is relative to the state of the society. Keynes put this point clearly: 'A great deal is at stake... we have to show that a *free system can be made to work*. To favour what is known as planning and management does not mean a falling away from the moral principles of liberty which could formerly be embodied in a simpler system...' [Harrod (1972); italics added]. The task of the modern societies is to find a delicate balance between individual freedom and social organization. A failure to achieve such a balance is sure to have disastrous consequences. This is even more true of the developing countries, where basic social institutions are much weaker than in the developed countries and less able to check the pulverising fall-out of individual greed.

Thus, a stock-taking of past failures and successes should convince us that, for all its shortcomings, the strategy of planned development has served the developing countries well. If, in the words of Lewis (1984), 'the viability of LDCs in normal times, like the 1950s and the 1960s, is now beyond doubt', the credit for pulling off this extraordinary feat must go to this time-tested 'mixed' development strategy. With the passage of time, the 'original' message has been modified and diluted to some extent, but this has happened within the framework of the accepted development philosophy. The recognition of the useful (supplementary) role that the market mechanism can play in the process of development is an especially important addition to the literature on development economics. There are many other aspects of the development process that must be recognized more explicitly within an (expanded) paradigm of development economics. Some of these are listed herein:

1. Thanks to the insights of development economics [such as, Sen (1981)] we now know better the 'dimensions' of the problems of poverty and starvation, especially in rural areas. It is clear that these problems need to be approached from both the demand side and the supply side. That the problem of extreme rural poverty can only be tackled within the context of a fast-growing agriculture, should now be accepted as an axiom. But, while this is a necessary condition, it is certainly not a sufficient condition for poverty reduction. To make an effective attack on rural poverty, additional steps must be taken to increase the income (effective demand) of the poor by keeping the prices of food reasonably low, and by arranging for appropriate employment-generating techniques of production.

2. Schultz (1981a), and others, have made clear the importance of investing in people's health and education. The important role that human capital, not just physical capital, plays in promoting economic development and technological change should be recognized more explicitly than before in development models and policies. These processes must be promoted and backed up by definite programmes to achieve universal education, especially technical education.

3. No country that made a success of economic development could ever have done so without first producing deep changes in the basic institutions of the society, especially those involving a redistribution of income and wealth. This has happened not only in socialist countries, but also in capitalistic countries. Harrod, in his classic biography of Keynes (1936), quotes him as saying that modern capitalistic institutions cannot be saved without capitalist societies accepting a substantial curtailment of the institution of private property and an increasing role of the state in economic management. Adelman and Morris (1973) show that substantial structural changes in the existing pattern of the distribution of wealth, along

with active egalitarian incrementalist policies, such as those proposed by Chenery (1975; 1983), are essential for reducing the unacceptable levels of economic inequalities found in the developing countries, and that without such changes taking place, the existing income inequalities will increase 'explosively' over time. Myrdal (1984), reviewing his thinking on development problems, concludes: 'What is needed to raise levels of living of the poor masses is radical institutional reforms. These would serve the double purpose of greater equality and economic growth.'

4. Self-serving definitions of equity, which seek to establish a correspondence between what an individual contributes to national income and what he receives from it, are not very helpful. As Tinbergen (1985) shows, 'equity means *equality of welfare* of all individuals concerned'. It is clearly recognized that 'historical' factors, especially the size of wealth and the stock of education that one has, determine the size of that individual's contribution to the wealth of nations.

However, to do all this, a visible role for the government in economic management must be accepted as a fact of life in the developing countries. For all his hesitation on this account, Lewis (1984) notes that 'what development economists cannot leave out of their calculations is the government's behaviour'. Obviously, it would be naive to think that the elites in the developing countries, whose economic interests are served by the existing institutions, would voluntarily accept substantial changes in those institutions. A decisive government action is required to make a dent in the status quo.

Simon (1983) has correctly observed that 'if we want an Invisible Hand to bring everything into some kind of social consonance, we should be sure, first, that our social institutions are framed to bring out our better selves, and second, that they do not require major sacrifices of self-interest by many people much of the time'. Unlike the developed countries, the developing countries have not, as a rule, succeeded in creating institutions which could ensure that the society did not continue to let only the poor to shoulder the major burden of economic development all the time. Without such an institutional bulwark against social exploitation of the poor, meaningful economic progress is not possible.

NOTES

[1]Among the dissenters, it is important to distinguish the economists whose main concern is about an appropriate 'form' of government intervention from the agnostics who would totally reject the government just because it is one!

[2]Samuelson (1976) points out that in a free economy where slavery is prohibited, 'a man is not even free to sell himself: he must *rent* himself at a wage'.

[3]As Haberler (1980) observes, this new nihilistic school 'is best known for the startling conclusions... to wit, that macro-economic policies, both monetary and fiscal, are ineffective, *even in the short run*... it is the extreme antithesis of orthodox Keynesianism.'

[4]This is not the consensus view now. In fact, the U.S. economy has been growing much more slowly—and that, too, when the markets are freer than in the Keynesian post-war era.

4

The Failure of Government as an Agent of Development

The market versus government issue requires further discussion as it has come to dominate all debate about development economics. It will be interesting to look at the matter by first examining Buchanan's (1986) anti-*dirigisme*, which has sought to put the government in the dock for its culpability for many an economic crime. Similar charges made by Friedman (1968), Lucas (1972), Becker (1983), and others have been reviewed in the previous chapter, but Buchanan has out-smarted the others in establishing his affiliation to Adam Smith. Buchanan's story of alleged government failure is of special interest for development theory and policy because of his invocation of public-choice theory in support of his anti-*dirigisme*. His discussion of the problem provides us with an altogether new viewpoint on the debate about the role of the market in the process of economic development.

It will be shown in this chapter that the public-choice theory does not provide any valid 'normative' or positive argument to justify the strictures passed by Buchanan against government. This can be substantiated by pin-pointing the limitations of the Pareto-optimality principle, the violation of which, to many neo-classical economists, is 'as if mother-hood is under cruel attack' [Sen (1984)]. It is also useful in this context to examine the relevance for development economics of other collective-choice rules—like the maximin criterion of Rawls (1971)—that focus explicitly on the question of social justice. Together with these, this analysis is enough to establish that the case for government failure to correct the inherent defects of the market mechanism does not rest on strong logical or moral foundations.

THE PHENOMENON OF MARKET FAILURE

This debate can be evaluated more clearly in the context of the literature on market failure. Every student of economics is familiar with Pigou's demonstration of 'market failure' to optimize social welfare in the presence of 'exter-nalities' in production or consumption. But the arguments by Friedman, Lucas, and Becker about government's failure to optimize social welfare are relatively recent and not so familiar. Thus, both these arguments need to be restated before proceeding to a re-examination of Buchanan's argument from the vantage-point of the public-choice theory.

Market Failure: Pigou and His Progeny

Pigou (1932) clearly spelt out the circumstances in which the market 'fails' to optimize social welfare and the implications this failure has for the government's behaviour. Briefly, the presence of external economies (and diseconomies) drives a wedge between marginal social and private benefits (and costs) and prevents the market from sending the right price signals to economic agents. Because of this lack of 'information', a regime of perfect competition fails to optimize social output. Under these circumstances, the government must, therefore, intervene in order to offset an inherent defect of the market. A more modern reformulation of the Pigovian position links market failure to a situation when market-clearing occurs 'without all mutually advantageous bargains having been struck' [Graaff (1989)]. This proviso is always satisfied when transaction costs, that is, the costs of getting all parties involved in a negotiated settlement, are positive.

Scitovsky (1954) has discussed at length the phenomenon of technological externalities in the context of developing countries.[1] He notes that, to the 'general rule' that the private profitability of investment is a reliable indicator of its social profitability, 'the exceptions are too great and obvious to be ignored, especially in underdeveloped countries....' He then concludes that 'the proper coordination of investment decisions would, therefore, require a signalling device to transmit information about present plans and future conditions as they are determined by present plans, and the pricing mechanism fails to provide this.'

The case of public goods illustrates the problem of market failure even more clearly. Public goods, for example, the operation of military establishments, the administration of justice, the provision of free education, have been defined by Musgrave (1959) as 'goods and services, whose inherent quality is such that they cannot be left to private enterprise'. According to Samuelson (1969), the central feature of a public good—characterized by joint supply and indivisibility—is that 'each individual's consumption leads to no subtraction from any other individual's consumption of that good'. But, because of this inherent plasticity of public good, it is in each individual's interest that all contribute to the production of such good, but that each individual would also be better off if only he did not pay for its consumption. Here we have the 'free rider' problem, that is, of the impossibility of excluding a person from the consumption of the (public) good through a market mechanism. This property makes it difficult to devise (voluntary) co-operative strategies to make the free rider pay for his 'lunch'. But, as Olson (1965) shows, when communities are large, voluntary co-operative agreements among individuals will not solve this problem, and the phenomenon of free riding will lead to the under-production of the public good. Government intervention is clearly indicated in such cases, which, however, does not necessarily prejudge the form and the mechanics of state intervention.

Chapter 3 examines at length the anti-government sentiments of some distinguished economists of the rational-expectationist school, like Friedman (1968), Lucas (1972), and others. But the rational-expectationists are not alone in their nihilism when it comes to assigning any constructive role to the government. Some development economists have also used anti-*dirigisme* as their trademark. Such economists maintain that government intervention is harmful even in cases where the market fails. Hence, according to them, a one-way shift from government control to free market is the only way to achieve both economic growth and equity, for the simple reason that government intervention is itself responsible for the less-than-full realization of these policy objectives.

The next to consider is Buchanan's 'normative' arguments for government failure, as Buchanan (1986) rests his anti-*dirigisme* on normative foundations, essentially the 'unanimity' principle. It is on the basis of such arguments that he harks the development economists back to Adam Smith.

Buchanan and Adam Smith

Buchanan advocates a research programme which is aimed to *'preserve a social order based on individual liberty'*, and insists that it can only be based on the Smithian utilitarian philosophy. Focusing on 'catallactics', the science of exchange, Buchanan pleads a return to Adam Smith, because this is the only way to have in full view the 'principle of spontaneous order, or spontaneous co-ordination, which is, as I have often suggested, perhaps the only real "principle" in economic theory as such'. For that reason, 'economics should concentrate more attention on market arrangements.' One may naturally ask, would such an overwhelming concern with market arrangements not be extraordinarily conservative? Buchanan does not think so, for the reason that 'choices in the market are not arbitrary, that there are narrow limits on the potential for exploitation of man by man, that markets tend to maximize freedom of persons from political control, (and) that liberty, which (is the) basic value, is best preserved in a regime that allows markets a major role.'

Within the Buchanan-Smith catallactic framework characterized by atomistic buyers and sellers, economic power becomes meaningless in perfect competitive markets. Buchanan, therefore, posits a normative judgement that 'voluntary exchange among persons is valued positively, while coercion is valued negatively; and hence the implication that the substitution of the former for the latter is desired....'

From this normative judgement, it is a short step to assert the 'failure' of the government, which appears to him to be exercising power to force a non-voluntary agreement among economic agents.

Buchanan and Tullock

Between Buchanan (1986) and Buchanan and Tullock (1962), there is a logical connection. The principle of unanimity based on the process of voluntary agreement among individuals is common to both economic and political processes. Buchanan and Tullock maintain that 'the individualistic theory of constitution we have been able to develop assigns a central role to a single decision-making rule—that of general consensus or unanimity....' According to Buchanan, the same single decision-making rule also applies to economics, as market processes can be construed as signifying unanimity about all kinds of market outcomes, even the socially unjust ones. This is because such outcomes can also be seen as symbolizing a lack of unanimity about changing an unjust state of the economy—since even one person can veto a 'just' change. In such a situation, according to the unanimity principle, the status quo would be the preferred outcome. It is quite another matter that what is preferred may not be the desired outcome demanded — at least not voluntarily — by the actual or potential voters in such situations.

Pareto-Optimality as a Collective-Choice Rule[2]

Buchanan's criticism of the *dirigiste* solutions to economic problems has one positive lesson for the development economist: it focuses his attention on the problem of selecting a collective-choice rule appropriate for a typical developing country. It is, indeed, odd that the literature on development economics has paid scant attention to the problems raised by the theory of collective choice in the context of maximizing social welfare. It is odd because in a mixed-economy framework, which does not take 'society' as an entity independent of its individual, it is of the utmost importance to look for reasonable and workable rules to relate in a non-dictatorial fashion individual preferences with social preferences—which is the subject-matter of the theory of collective choice.

The only collective-choice rule that has apparently been accepted, though only implicitly, by some development economists is the Pareto-optimality principle.[3] But a total acceptance of this principle chains development economics exclusively to market solutions—leaving little room for a mixed economy or the search for equitable arrangements. The anti-*dirigiste* 'temper' of the rule follows from the Fundamental Theorem of Welfare Economics, which establishes a two-way link between competitive equilibrium and the Pareto Optimum (Chapter 5). Thus, if efficiency is the only objective, and/or if equity considerations are dominated by it, government intervention is redundant because an economy in competitive equilibrium is, by definition, 'unimprovable', because it is also Pareto-optimal. If the attainment of Pareto-optimality is a necessary condition to maximize social welfare, then free markets, powered only by the utility-maximizing egoistic individuals, would surely achieve such a social objective.

However, if Pareto-optimality should become the ultimate social objective to be aimed at (and much of modern welfare economics is based on such a weird premise), then that woebegone society will have in store for its members, especially the poorer ones, a very parsimonious feast.[4] This is because an economy at Pareto Optimum could carry on with a good conscience even if those who are deprived of the basic necessities of life, such as food, cannot be made better-off without depriving, even modestly, the rich of their 'hard-earned' wealth (or income). Another property of such an elitist state of bliss is that the society is indifferent to the multiplicity of Pareto Optimum points along a given contract curve. This is another way of saying that such a state signifies unanimity— a property central to Buchanan and Tullock's *Calculus of Consent*. Can such a state be called a state of bliss in any meaningful sense of the term? The answer would be in the negative because Pareto-optimality points are neutral with respect to any reasonable distributional considerations.

The rule is deficient; it does not work in the presence of externalities. A typical case, discussed above, is that of public good where the free rider cannot be excluded from his consumption through the market mechanism. Since, in this case, it is in everybody's interest to understate the benefits one expects from the consumption of such a good, a public project producing it will be defeated in an open election even though it will maximize social welfare. Since the provision of public goods is a crucial element of the investment programmes in the developing countries, Pareto-optimality typically will lead to lower growth as well as to a lower equity.

DECISION RULES WITH A CONSCIENCE

The Pareto rule is not a universally true principle of collective choice which retains its validity irrespective of the nature of the society. Indeed, as we will discuss presently, there are other collective-choice rules which should be more acceptable to the development economist, because considerations of growth as well as equity are even more important in the developing countries than in the developed ones, owing to the fragile social institutions of the former. (This is not to assert that Pareto-optimality is any more relevant a decision-making rule in the developed countries than in the developing countries.) Another important point in the present context is that even a voluntary, but passive, acceptance of Pareto-optimality does not guarantee that it would be endorsed if other more acceptable collective-choice rules were also available.

Let us now turn to a consideration of alternative choice rules which may be more relevant for development economics because of their emphasis on the element of morality in an individual's behaviour and the emphasis on the right kind of institutions. There are many such rules, which are discussed at length in Mueller (1979) and Sen (1970), but only two of them are presented here.

Harsanyi's Social Welfare Function

Within the utilitarian framework that underlies the Pareto principle, Harsanyi (1977; 1977a) proves the result that social welfare is a function of the weighted average of individual welfare. The remarkable aspect of Harsanyi's proof is that, unlike the Pareto principle, it explicitly achieves the result on normative grounds. The motivation of Harsanyi's research is to provide an insight into how collective decisions ought to be made. To this end, Harsanyi postulates that the individual's preferences are divisible into personal preferences, and moral or social preferences. In making known his moral preferences, an individual is supposed to reflect the preferences of every other individual by putting himself in the position of the other individual. The high point of Harsanyi's utilitarian model is his success in deriving a social welfare function as a weighted average of the individual utilities. The additive form of the welfare function denotes the highly individualistic motivation of the model—namely, that *every* individual's welfare matters.[5]

Two points should be noted here. First, the Harsanyi individuals are not the exclusively egotistic individuals with

Paretian idiosyncrasies. Instead, they are also moral individuals who wish to make their decisions in an impartial fashion. Second, if the world is such that the Harsanyi individual's decisions carry a significant weight, as opposed to those of the Paretian individuals, then this world is very different from Adam Smith's world or the one that Buchanan prefers. It may be noted that this is not the world where the Invisible Hand of the market is the only purveyor of the good things of life—or strictly speaking, of a specific (weighted) sum of *utilities* of goods.

Rawlsian Collective-Choice Rule

Unlike the Pareto rule, Rawls (1971) rejects utilitarian philosophy and the social-welfare-function approach based on this philosophy.[6] The most distinguishing feature of the Rawlsian analysis, which makes it especially attractive to the development economist, is its insistence on the creation and establishment of just (and progressive) institutions relating to the 'basic structure of the society'. Within the framework of such institutions, collective decision-making will ensure a just 'assignment of fundamental rights and duties', and a morally right 'division of advantages from social co-operation'. Unlike the Paretian approach, which condones actual welfare losses of some if these can be compensated—but only notionally, not actually— by the potential gains of others, the Rawlsian theory does not allow for such trade-offs as socially meaningful or desirable: 'Justice denies that the loss of freedom for some is made right by a greater good shared by others.' Instead, the theory insists that the needs of the least-privileged individuals in the society, measured by an adequate supply of 'primary goods,' must be satisfied first. These primary goods are identified as the 'basic rights and liberties, powers and opportunities, income and wealth'.

The Rawlsian framework is based on two analytically

related but separable principles. The first is the fundamental notion of 'justice as fairness,' which requires that individuals choose just rules from a hypothetical 'original position' of complete equality. Analytically speaking, this 'original position' is reached by stepping through a 'veil of ignorance' that hides from the individuals in the original position all the advantages that may accrue to them from their own decisions. This analytical procedure highlights the basic importance of impartiality for ensuring that the rules of justice so chosen are 'fair'.

Two fundamental principles of justice flow from this position of primordial equality:

(a) 'Each person is to have an equal right to most extensive basic liberty compatible with a similar liberty for others' and

(b) 'Inequalities are arbitrary unless it is reasonable to expect that they work for everybody's advantage, and provided that the positions and offices to which they attach, or from which they may be gained, are open to all.' Rawls's aim is to find out just institutions and distinguish them from unjust ones and, in that context, he seeks to maximize in a lexicographic fashion the welfare of the worst-off individuals in the society. (For more details, see Chapter 5.)

IS MORALITY A VIRTUE?

The public-choice perspective also helps to focus our attention on such basic issues as the limits of individual liberty and the place of moral and ethical perceptions in development philosophy.

The Priority of Liberty

Buchanan's impassioned case for the free markets is based on his *'faith* that an understanding of the price system offered the best possible avenue for the generation of support for free institutions' (italics added). It is only through such an understanding that we can 'preserve order based on individual liberty.' Thus, in Buchanan's view, individual liberty is accorded priority over all other social and economic imperatives—like ensuring equality in income and wealth and providing basic amenities of life to the least privileged in the society. (As noted above, a similar view is implicit in the Paretian principle.) Buchanan deepens the normative colour of his argument by emphasizing that voluntary agreements reached through the markets are the only preservers of individual liberty, and that the involuntary agreements reached through government meddling always compromise individual liberty. This line of argument suffers from a fatal flaw, which is that it defines specific market arrangements as voluntary or involuntary according to whether they are made through the market (the former) or by the government (the latter). It proceeds to derive from this definition the conclusion that market arrangements are superior to those made by the government. This is not a logical result at all, but simply a restatement of a definition.

In Rawls's view, a central importance is attached to maximizing the welfare of the least-privileged classes of the society—viz., those who have less access to primary goods than others. This view, according to Rawls, is consistent with the priority he ascribes to liberty. In addition to his two basic principles of justice, Rawls makes the following important point: 'Now the basis for the priority of liberty is roughly as follows: as the conditions of civilization improve, the marginal significance for our good of further economic and social advantages diminishes relative to the interest of liberty....'

In this perception, as Mueller (1979) points out, Rawls sees 'liberty essentially as a luxury good in each individual's preference function.' The implication of such an approach is that individual liberty is a 'consequence' of a restructuring of the basic institutions of the society in such a way that the needs of the least privileged are met first. In other words, individual liberty is defined as incorporating a system of rights in such a manner that it is preserved, indeed maximized, if as a result of the working of social and political institutions the entitlement to primary goods of the least privileged are met—no matter what else is met—in all states of the economy. (See also Chapter 5).

The Importance of Moral Values

That part of the literature on development economics which claims to be truly positivistic and 'value-free' is, without doubt, barking up the wrong tree. This is because even the so-called 'objective' statements made on the strength of Paretian philosophy, which is assumed to reflect the principle of unanimity, do involve a moral judgement.[7] Thus, there is no need, in the name of scientific rectitude, to rid development economics of ethical and moral norms and values. Indeed, scientific rectitude, according to Hume's Law, requires that a community should have evolved the concepts of right and wrong in order to be able to make propositions about what ought to be done, and to derive any prescriptive conclusions from empirical findings. It is this shared conceptualization of what is right and wrong that should guide the development economist in choosing morally acceptable collective-choice rules as a basis of social policy.

Equally reprehensible for the development economist should be the non-consequentialistic 'entitlement principle of distribution' spelled out by Nozick (1974). According to him, certain values—such as, individual liberty—should be

upheld for their own sake, and not judged by social consequences. (See Chapter 5 for more details).

One outcome of the Nozickian non-consequentialism is
that the government is not allowed to specify what a person
should or should not have— that would make it look too
'nosy'. It should, instead, restrict itself to specifying only the
procedures that make actual individual holdings—for instance,
private property—legitimate. But such a view is not acceptable.
For if sticking to procedures makes one unmindful of the
social consequences of a certain structure of property rights,
even though they be legitimate, then these procedures, indeed
the entire approach to the problem, must be revised. If,
according to Nozick's principle, it does not matter how happiness comes about, what the sources of a given state of happiness are, and how that happiness is shared, whether grabbed
by a few or distributed more widely, then, surely, something
is very wrong with our social vision.

THE QUESTION OF RELEVANCE

The public-choice perspective shows that the debates now
rocking development economics—about freeing it from the
clutches of a sterile government that invariably 'fails' to
deliver, about making it more 'scientific' by letting it
metamorphose into a neo-classical economics which obeys
Pareto-optimality like a Divine Law, and about emptying it
of any remnants of ethical and moral concern—are really
non-debates. These debates are not even 'scientific', because
they fail to recognize the central importance of a widely
accepted system of moral values for making scientific statements. They are also myopic because they stick to only one
decision-making rule—viz., Pareto-optimality—which is un-
repentantly neutral with respect to various states of the

distribution of income and wealth. The works of such distinguished economists as Wicksell (1958), Rawls (1971), Harsanyi (1977), and many others emphasize the need for a contractarian-cum-utilitarian framework to make the process of collective decision-making work. These approaches either presuppose the need for creating just institutions (the utilitarian approach) or explicitly stipulate the need for creating just institutions (the contractual approach). Both these approaches have the merit of prescribing rules and issuing directions for an optimal working of the government. The works of economists like Becker (1983) have further deepened our understanding of how the government works to correct market failures, even when it is seen as competing for political favours from the vested interests in the society.

As I have emphasized up to now, there is more to development economics than a mere prescription for blind adherence to the rules of the free market. With its normative props removed, the market arrangements look highly vulnerable and prone to 'failure' when it comes to a restructuring of the basic institutions of the society to ensure social justice. By the same token. Buchanan's claim of the innate failure of the government turns out, on normative grounds alone, to be without any normative or 'positive' foundation.

It is crucial for a continued vitality of development economics as a discipline to explicitly recognize that there is more than one collective-choice rule which can be used as a basis for translating individual preferences into social preferences, and that such rules are deeply coloured by the ethical and moral norms widely shared by the society. It should also be understood that an intelligent evaluation of these rules is only possible through an understanding of their relativity to the nature of the society. *There is no such thing as an ideal or sure-fire system of collective-choice rules that works equally well at all times, in all societies, and for every possible configuration of individuals' preferences.*

The aim of development economics must be to understand the successes and failures of the market and the government in the wider context of social justice in a growing economy. But social justice can only be achieved by creating institutions which can transmute the longing for a better world into a set of policies that aim at changing the status quo in the developing countries. It should be clearly understood in this connection that if an outcome—for instance, one particular outcome of the workings of the market—gains wide acceptance and is not openly questioned, it does not necessarily make it desirable. In a world marked with extreme poverty, a tacit acceptance of the status quo is hardly ever a sign of its endorsement.

If we propagate the great virtues of individual freedom that market arrangements allegedly signify, then we must honestly reflect on whether it is freedom for only a privileged few or freedom for all. The litmus test that all theories and institutions should pass should establish their contribution to and relevance for ensuring social justice. The Rawlsian homily to social philosophers is apt: 'A theory, however elegant and economical, must be rejected or revised if it is untrue; likewise, laws and institutions, no matter how efficient, must be reformed or abolished if they are unjust'.

NOTES

[1]A technological externality may be defined as 'the indirect effect of a consumption activity or a production activity on the consumption set of a consumer, the utility function of a consumer, or the production function of a producer' [Laffont (1989)]. A related concept is that of pecuniary externality— that is, one that works through the price system; but the relevant definition is the one that relates to a technological externality which defines a market failure.

[2]If there are states of economy a and b, and there is at least one person who prefers a to b while everyone else is indifferent to both a and b, then

a is Pareto-wise superior to *b*. Pareto-optimality is satisfied if in set A there is no alternative which is Pareto-wise better than *a*. On this definition, everyone in the society is indifferent to both *a* and *b*. See Sen (1970a).

[3]Indeed, some development economists consider this principle as an alternative to development economics. For instance, Lal (1983) recommends that the allocational principles of welfare economics, based on the principle of Pareto-optimality, should replace development economics because of the observed 'failure' of the *dirigiste* prescriptions of the latter.

[4]However, the Pareto-optimality rule takes on a relatively more 'benign' look when interpreted as a 'core' or a 'value'—in that these formulations stipulate a perfect redistribution of property rights [Khan (1991)]. But the equity credentials of the rule become suspect once equity is defined in a more natural sense, a la Rawls, of the redistribution of property rights and income in accordance with the needs of the least-privileged in society.

[5]A multiplicative form would not achieve this result because it would give a life-and-death power to an individual who wishes to wipe out the preferences of the other individuals in the society by simply assigning a zero value to social outcome.

[6]Rawls's work is perhaps the most complete modern exposition of the contractarian philosophy of Rousseau, Kant and many others.

[7]As Sen (1970*a*) points out, 'unanimous value judgements may provide the basis of a great deal of welfare economics, but this is not so because these are not value judgements, but because these judgements are acceptable to all.'

5

Moral Values and
Development Economics

W hile elaborating on certain themes already outlined, I
wish to argue that development economics in its next growth
cycle must seek a creative symbiosis of ethics and economics
which can avoid both the Scylla of anti-moralist oblivion and
the Charybdis of a non-consequentialist morality. In such
delicate steering, development economics must be based on

a meaningful consequentialist moral-economic philosophy. It would be illuminating for development economics to view the justness of the basic institutions—social, economic and political—as linked both to the maximization of the welfare of the least-privileged individuals in society and to a net reduction in their numbers. Such a development philosophy has a clear political dimension: it should help create, in the words of Rawls (1985), an 'overlapping consensus' about the aim and direction of the development process. To this end, it would seem natural for development economics to break out of its anti-ethical shell and live normally, without losing its soul or scientific content, in a world where 'rationality' cannot meaningfully be taken as a synonym for self-interest, and where moral concern for others would not count as a sure sign of irrationality. It would also be a natural thing for development economics to opt for an ethical stance that is sensitive to the consequences of the exercise of specific individual rights.

TIME FOR REFLECTION

The time is not yet ripe for development economists to bathe in the warm glow of self-congratulation, even though the essence of the message of development economics remains intact. The fact is that at least partly in response to the anti-*dirigiste*'s attack, development economics has relinquished some vital territory: the 'invisible hand' (the market) has been allowed to win for itself a greater role than was envisaged by the pioneers of the discipline, and much less visible now than in the past are some of its key concepts—for instance, the strategies of 'balanced' or 'unbalanced' growth [Nurkse (1953); Hirschman (1958)], 'unequal development' between the centre and the periphery [Amin (1976)], the 'big push'

Development Economics

[Rosenstein-Rodan (1943)], 'great spurt' [Gerschenkron (1962)], 'minimum critical effort' [Galenson and Leibenstein (1955)], 'stages of growth' [Rostow (1971)], 'backward and forward linkages' [Hirschman (1958)], and 'unlimited supplies of labour' [Lewis (1954)].

As a result of such vital concessions, development economics may appear to have lost some of its lustre. Yet what seems to some to be a retreat from strategic high ground may simply have been the result of more learning on the part of development economists: a greater realization of the deficiencies of the government as a regulator of the economic tides, and a clearer understanding of the role of international trade and international migration in the development process. The fact of the matter is that many of the key insights of the discipline have survived the cauldron of controversy. As discussed in Chapters 3 and 4, apropos the market versus the government debate, neither in theory nor in practice have things gone as badly for the government as some distinguished rational-expectationists [Lucas (1972)] would have liked. Development plans are still in vogue in developing countries, despite warnings to the contrary by agnostics among development economists [Bauer (1972)]. No-Plan periods are still considered an oddity in the annals of policy-making, and the problems of poverty, inequality, and income redistribution continue to concern both theorists and policy-makers in developing countries. While economic growth has been healthy in most of the developing countries—indeed, it has been remarkable in NICs [Little (1982); Bhagwati (1984)],—not all the credit for this success goes to the magic of the 'invisible hand', since the visible hand of the state has also been beneficial for society.

In view of the nature of the debate, the task of strengthening the foundations of development economics as a new paradigm—or, to use the terminology of Lakatos (1970), a Progressive Scientific Research Programme—is large and challenging. (See Chapters 1 and 2.) There is some truth in the observation that development economics has shown considerable vulnerability to the 'unlikely conjunction of distinct ideological currents', and that 'no new synthesis has appeared' to meet the criticism of the Left and the Right [Hirschman (1981*b*)]. Hence, to meet the many new intellectual challenges— to thrive, and not just to survive and exist—the conceptual foundations of development economics need to be laid down more clearly than in the past. In order to accomplish that, development economics must go through some kind of a purgatory to lose at least some of its impurities. Our discipline need not continue to be a net borrower of ideas from neo-classical economics.[1] It should throw fresh light on old questions and offer new hypotheses of its own—especially in areas wherein lies its comparative advantage: namely, in striking a happy balance between the relative roles of the market and the government, in better explaining the processes of growth and structural change, in understanding more clearly the causes of the inequalities of income and wealth between the rich and the poor, and in finding the many ways of curing the lot of the worst-off individuals in society. This, of course, is a tall order.

To implement such a research programme would require the exploration, among other things, of the complex relationship between production and exchange, especially of the wage goods in relation to the 'entitlements' of the least privileged groups in society. Equally important, the genesis and structure of private property rights, especially in land-holdings, must be evaluated by reference to the universally held ideas of justice and fairness, and such vital issues should also be related to their economic, social, and political consequences. It is precisely on issues like these that the inadequacies are most striking—of a so-called value-free economics on which development economics draws so heavily, and of the non-consequentialist moral philosophy, which both neo-classical economics and development economics have so far ignored. These inadequacies must be supplied by focusing development economics on a wider analytical perspective of individual behaviour. What is needed is a view of human motivation which does not rely exclusively on self-interest maximization, but which also models economic agents as responding as much to moral values—like impartiality, universality, sympathy, commitment—as to egotistical drives. On the other hand, development economics must also model a consequence-sensitive view of moral rights, which should nevertheless be seen as possessing an intrinsic value and not merely an instrumental value.

As pointed out in Chapter 4, development economics should pay attention to the vast though somewhat difficult area of public-choice theory, which tells us that there are not one but several rules—made by, among others, the government, social organizations, labour unions, business—to relate 'the individual to a collectivity' [Arrow (1977)]. There is another reason why development economics must be reconstructed from this particular viewpoint. The public-choice theory emphasizes that individual preferences and their 'contents' are themselves shaped by the nature of the society.[2] The essential relativity, plurality and comprehensiveness of collective-choice rules are exactly the features which development economics needs to acquire to secure its existence as a paradigm and enhance its theoretical rigour and practical relevance.

To set the stage for the subsequent discussion, the next two sections are devoted to a consideration of the reasons for relating economic thinking to the universally accepted ethical mores in a society and to the relevant choice rules which aim at marrying economics to ethics. Some of these issues have been raised to analyse the market-government debate, but here the motivation is to examine the broader issue of what the moral foundations of development economics are. One negative aspect of this issue is the irrelevance from the point of view of development economics of that strand of thinking which condones and even preaches the immorality of moral rights. One important aspect of this immorality is the right of the privileged few to perpetuate the status quo with respect to an unjust state of the economy.

LEARNING TO STAND IN SOMEONE ELSE'S SHOES

It is widely alleged that anti-ethicalism was preached by Adam Smith, who laid down the maxim: 'It is not from the benevolence of the butcher, the brewer, or the baker, that we expect our dinner, but from their regard to their own interests' [Smith (1975), pp. 26-27]. Adam Smith, who also wrote the *Theory of Moral Sentiments,* has probably been misunderstood as issuing a call against relying on moral principles to explain the mysteries of the economic processes.[3] It was left to Robbins (1932) to put economics into a positivist box, immune to ethical clamouring.[4] According to this line of thought, rational behaviour is taken as a synonym for self-interest-maximization and, indeed, any activity other than maximizing self-interest is considered to be irrational.

Selfishness and the Status Quo

The strongest plea for the status quo is the Pareto-optimality rule. Any existing state will, for instance, be Pareto-optimal if the condition of the poor cannot be made better without worsening the living standards of the rich! The anti-change property of the rule springs from its neutrality with respect to the distribution of income and wealth, however unequal may be the gap between the rich and the poor. This result will follow if, as is the practice, all Pareto-optimal points are declared as indifferent. The fact that it signifies 'unanimity' does not make the rule any less conservative. The mere fact that a given state of affairs is accepted sullenly by the poor does not necessarily mean that it is also endorsed by them, because the political and social forces that sustain such a state may not have their active support. Such seeming endurance of an undesirable state of affairs will vanish on the appearance of the first ray of hope of changing the people's uneventful survival.

The inherent conservatism of Pareto-optimality is also highlighted by the so-called Fundamental Theorem of Welfare Economics: 'Every competitive equilibrium is Pareto-optimal; and, with a non-distortionary redistribution of initial endowments, every Pareto-optimal state is also a competitive equilibrium state.' The first part of the theorem proves that competitive equilibrium is efficient.[5] Thus, if competitive equilibrium co-exists with extreme poverty, then nothing can be done about it. However, as pointed out by Sen (1987), the second part of the theorem carries the seeds of change: it says that, *for some initial endowments,* the Pareto-optimal state will also approximate a competitive equilibrium, indicating a correction of the sub-optimal initial endowment patterns, which may be biased against the poor before the market takes over its allocative functions. But such a happy confluence will follow only if people voluntarily furnish information about the initial endowment—a condition that is seldom satisfied. At any rate, most neo-classical economists would consider such an interpretation of the theorem as reading too much in the tea leaves.

Altruism and Social Change

Fortunately, the progeny of Adam Smith have not been too

completely lacking in imagination to see that 'rational' behaviour need not be—indeed, is not—antiseptically self-centred welfarism, which is what positive economics demands, and which development economics has tended to accept without question. Aristotle's homily—'we should behave to our friends as we would wish our friends to behave to us'— has not been entirely lost on economists. The central thrust of such arguments and proposed rules of behaviour is that selfish behaviour alone is not an adequate description of real life. This is because the rule of law, based on equity and justice, is essential to prevent free markets—which are invariably fed by asymmetric information—from working against the interests of a civilised society. The same qualification would apply to the somewhat starry-eyed view that it is altruism alone that makes the world go round. In general, it is always a happy mixture of selfish and selfless behaviours which has accounted for success in the real world.[6]

Sidgwick's (1874) principle of 'equity' requires that 'whatever action any of us judges to be right for himself, he implicitly judges right for all similar persons in similar circumstances.' Harsanyi's (1977) 'equiprobability model for moral value judgement', briefly described in the previous chapter, also requires that the individual possesses not only personal preferences but also *moral* preferences. These moral preferences 'guide his thinking in those—possibly very rare—moments when he forces a special impersonal and impartial attitude, that is, a moral attitude, upon himself.' Hare (1963) equates equity with the property of universality of personal preferences, emphasizing that the individual's rational behaviour should not differ when acting in 'similar circumstances'. The key insights of the model are that individuals are motivated to action both for personal and moral reasons, and that every individual's welfare matters. While personal preferences are guided by the self-interest-maximization rule, moral preferences reflect the Harsanyi individual's capacity to make an impartial moral value judgement by putting himself into another individual's position. The criterion for evaluating a value judgement as a moral one is to postulate that it is not 'unduly influenced by one's personal interests and personal preferences' [Harsanyi (1977), p. 636].

Unlike the Harsanyi rule, the Rawlsian choice-rule rejects utilitarianism. As shown in Chapter 4, this rule is expressed in terms of the concept of 'justice as fairness.' The concept is based on the notion that free and equal citizens of a society 'do not view the social order as a fixed natural order, or as an institutional hierarchy justified by religious or aristocratic values' [Rawls (1985)]. Therefore, if the existing social order does not accord with the universally accepted notion of justice in a society, the social order can be, and indeed must be, changed. These changes will take place as part of a system of (voluntary) cooperation between free and equal persons 'who are born into the society in which they live' and (mentally) pass through the 'veil of ignorance' to make impartial decisions—from the 'original position'—about the basic 'structure' of the society. What these persons in the original position maximize is the welfare of the 'worst-off' individuals in society. The thrust of the Rawlsian criterion is to find just institutions which are chosen 'fairly'. It also implies an activist public policy which aims to *correct* the injustices of existing institutions. In this sense, unlike the Pareto-optimality rule, the Rawlsian rule is not status quoist.

Another aspect of the Rawlsian conception which should make it especially attractive to development economics is that it is not a metaphysical but a 'moral conception worked out for... political, economic and social institutions' [Rawls (1985)]. Being essentially a politically-oriented conception, it emphasizes the need for creating an 'overlapping consensus', which includes 'all the opposing philosophical and religious doctrines likely to persist in a democratic society'. Such an 'overlapping consensus' should be forged mainly by emphasizing active poverty alleviation programmes, which aim to reduce absolute poverty within the context of a growing economy. It is essential to guarantee social unity, which, according to Rawls, denotes 'the allegiance of citizens to their common institutions' based on their 'public acceptance of a political conception of justice to regulate the basic structure of the society.'

With the Rawlsian conception of justice, we have come a long way from the Paretian insistence on the maximization of utilities, and on individual selfishness as the hallmark of rational behaviour. In this model, we have ' free and equal individuals,' who think about the welfare of other persons, especially of the worst-off individual in society. The sole aim is to restructure the basic social, political and economic institutions which have a direct bearing on the individual's well-being and social welfare. Such a laudable aim may not be utility-maximizing at all, because structural change will, in general, cause disutility to those adversely affected by such change.

ON THE IMMORALITY OF MORAL 'RIGHTS'

An important aspect of introducing ethics into development economics is to put at our disposal the philosophical analyses which accord priority to moral 'rights' and freedoms—that is, certain rights must be respected for what they are and be exercised irrespective of their (utilitarian) consequences. But a moment's reflection should show that the exercise of rights, especially the rights of private property, has a profound effect on the basic structure of society. It is, therefore, a crucial question whether development theory needs a strictly non-consequentialist view of ethics. The answer is probably in the negative. While rights do have an intrinsic value, they cannot be held without a sensitivity to their economic and social consequences.

It is instructive to consider the question of the priority of 'rights' with reference to Nozick's moral entitlement theory to highlight the limitations of an extremist view of non-consequentialist moral theories. It is easy to see that an insensitive non-consequentialism can turn 'moral' rights into crass immorality.

Nozickian Theory of Entitlement

Nozick (1974) offers a theory of entitlement and 'historical justice'. The theory is strictly non-consequentialist and procedural. While holdings acquired through illegitimate means, such as theft, are not just, Nozick sanctifies with the attribute of justice any existing distribution of holdings that is based on legitimate procedures regarding the structure of property rights:

> The general outlines of the theory of justice in holdings are that the holdings of a person are just if he is entitled to them by the principles of justice in acquisition and transfer, or by the principle of rectification of justice (as specified by the first two principles). If each person's holdings are just, then the total set (distribution) of holdings is just.

Nozick explicitly recognizes that 'past injustices' may shape 'present holdings in various ways'. He also recognizes, though only in a footnote, that 'if the principle of rectification of violations of the first two principles [the principle of justice in acquisition and transfer] yields more than one description of holdings, then some choice must be made as to which of these is to be realized. Perhaps the sort of considerations about distributive justice and equity that I argue against play a legitimate role in *this* subsidiary choice.' (Italics in original.)

Having made this important observation, Nozick does not pursue the all-important question of the rectification of past injustices in acquisition, perhaps because he considers it a 'subsidiary choice'. Instead, he specifically rules out any 'patterning' of the existing structure of property rights—such as, through deliberate government action—since doing so would constitute a violation of the individual's rights: 'From the point of view of an entitlement theory, redistribution is a serious matter indeed, involving as it does the violation of people's rights'. If accepted, such a procedural view of distributive justice would, for instance, rule out taking any corrective action against the feudal structures of landholding found in many developing countries today just because the ownership titles were transferred legally—even though, as in India and Pakistan, many such transfers were made by a colonial government to their local collaborators as a reward for their 'unsocial' services. According to Nozick, such corrective action cannot be justified on egalitarian grounds, because 'past circumstances or actions of people can create differential entitlements or differential deserts to things', and are, therefore, morally justified.

Obviously, Nozickian non-consequentialism would not be acceptable either from a moral or an economic point of view. A dramatic illustration of the immorality, and also of the inefficiency, of strict non-consequentialism is provided by the incidence of famines, which, in certain cases, are a direct result of a legitimate exercise of legitimate property rights, and of the defence by the state of such rights.[7] The problem with the Nozick-type argument is that it views freedom as strictly negative: it takes the form of constraints on individual action only—so that nothing can be done to stop the individuals from enjoying their legitimate rights. Nozick rules out taking positive action to correct the consequences of an individual indulging his rights. This is a counter-intuitive argument. One would normally think it natural to be sensitive to the consequences of specific states and to take positive steps to guard moral rights if these states are threatened. This would be true even if one rejects the

115

strict consequentialism of the utilitarian philosophy, which judges the rightness of specific actions solely by the goodness of the consequences.

ON THE BENEVOLENCE OF THE BUTCHER, THE BREWER, AND THE BAKER

There are numerous examples to illustrate the need for a clear (consequentialist) ethical vision to comprehend most of the central economic problems in the developing countries. What Robbins calls 'valuation and obligations' intermingle with 'ascertainable facts' to produce acceptable solutions for such issues. In other words, pure selfishness should be combined with 'benevolence' to make an adequate model for the world.

The Poverty Issue

Let us first consider the problem of (absolute) poverty, which in the extreme case takes the form of famine. Sen (1984) demonstrates that the tools of neo-classical economics are completely inadequate to analyse this problem. This is because, as Koopmans (1957) points out, it assumes that 'each consumer can, if necessary, survive, on the basis of the resources he holds and direct use of labour, without engaging in exchange, and still have something to spare of some type of labour which is sure to meet with a positive price in any equilibrium.' Thus, the efficiency-oriented analyses of poverty (and famine), which focus only on the metric of *food availability* to model the 'survival' requirement, may be seriously misleading. The fact of the matter is that famines have occurred in (efficient) situations where food availability was not the problem. The villain of the piece in most cases has been the widespread 'entitlement' failure of the poor—due, for example, to the inflation of food prices—which, in turn, entails the denial of an elementary freedom to them.

The poverty problem cannot be analysed with the help of the non-consequentialist moral rights theories either. For example, the (moral) question of the 'priority' of private property rights is related to the prevalence of the feudal structure of landholding, the title to which is acquired and transferred by the owners legally. But the very existence of such legal structures may, in some cases, be the root cause of extreme poverty, even of famine, in developing countries. It follows that an adequate resolution of this problem will require that development economics recognize the inter-dependence of production and distribution of food (or, the efficiency argument), and that, in addition, re-examine the moral aspect of property rights—an immoral albeit *legitimate* exercise of which may contribute to the perpetuation of extreme poverty and deprivation (or, the moral argument). Here, more than anywhere else, the very 'existence' of development economics depends on its ability to recognize the moral aspects of the problem.

On Reducing Inequality

Next to absolute poverty, the problem of inequality—in other words, the economic or social position of an individual in relation to the other individuals—is one of the most important basic issues that development economics is concerned with. The 'quality' of economic growth is judged by reference to its effect on the degree of inequality —measured by such indices as the Gini coefficient. Widening inequalities, even when associated with improvement in the lot of the poor, are considered politically unacceptable, partly because of the 'envy' factor. Yet both the efficiency-oriented economic analyses and the non-consequentialist moral rights theories make light of the problem. The reason for this apathy is an insufficient understanding of the relation of the inequality problem to the consequentialist ethicalism.

To help ourselves see the problem clearly, let us note at the outset that the Rawlsian (maximin) principle of 'justice as fairness' is not a principle of equality—even though the two are related in spirit if not in words. The reason is that in recommending an improvement in the welfare of the worst-off individual(s) in all states of the economy, Rawls's principle does not put limits on the extent of simultaneous endeavour to improve the lot of the best-off in the same society. Thus, the Rawlsian criterion of justness may be consistent with a situation in which relatively small efforts to improve the welfare of the worst-off individual(s) are accompanied by immense favour towards the best-off, thereby widening the gap between the two! Hence, as Tullock (1986) points out, 'the maximin principle of justice [as fairness] is *not* a plausible principle of *equality,* for whether or not such an alteration in a society's institutions would make that more *just,* it would certainly not make it better with respect to inequality'. (Italics in original.) He also dismisses the Rawlsian principle as a principle of redistribution, 'because the Rawls's [sic] method surely would lead to less income redistribution than we now have.' However, this criticism is only valid in so far as the Rawlsian maximin principle is not necessarily inequality-reducing. It follows that, to be relevant from the point of view of income redistribution, the Rawlsian maximin principle of justice should be made consistent with a maximin principle of equality. How can this be done? Temkin (1986) suggests that the trick is to link the degree of inequality in different states of the economy to the position of the worst-off individual(s) in those states with respect to inequality, and to stipulate that, for one state of the economy to be worse than the other, the welfare of the worst-off individuals(s) must be in a worse condition, within that state.

It may be noted that the stipulation mentioned becomes

relevant only if the level of welfare of the worst-off groups is the same in alternative states of the economy. The intuitive meaning of this somewhat complex formulation is, however, quite clear: 'the maximin principle of equality would first have us maximize the relative position of the worst-off group, and then minimize the number of people in that group, as long as we were not thereby increasing the complaint of the remaining members of the worst-off group' [Temkin (1986)].

Once the problem is defined in this way—relating inequality to the maximization of the lot of the worst-off individuals, and to the minimization of the number of persons so situated—it dispels much of the confusion surrounding the 'reasons for redistribution', which Tullock (1986) decries as 'chaotic'. He finds these reasons as unacceptable —indeed, hypocritical—partly because he thinks that 'most people in discussing income distribution are extremely charitable. It is the amount they actually give away which is modest,' and partly because 'most of the (income) transfers in most societies, democratic or dictatorial, do not go to the poor. They go to people who for one reason or another are politically well-organized'. There is some weight in Tullock's argument because it is mostly the politically vocal middle class, and not so much the voiceless poor, who get the most from income transfers caused by the state-sponsored social-security pro-grammes. But this is not necessarily an argument for dismissing the issue, as Tullock does, but to rest the rationale for redis-tribution on moral grounds. Also, the 'fact' that charity is inadequate, or that it does not reach the poor cannot be used to argue against increasing the volume of charity or ensuring that it does reach the target group.

Competition, Cooperative Action, and Distributive Justice

A direct outcome of the anti-moralist, efficiency-oriented

analyses of growth has been their exclusive emphasis on 'competition' as the only form of economic activity through which both private gain and social product are maximized. The importance of cooperative action is recognized in certain game-theoretic situations, but seldom as a star performer.[8] The non-consequentialist moral-rights theories also eulogize the competitive solution on the ground that it preserves individual freedom. Not only that: in Nozick-type analyses this solution is considered superior to any other solution, even to one based on a cooperative strategy.

The case of the Prisoner's Dilemma has been used to illustrate the shortcomings of 'strictly dominant' individualistic strategies, which lead each of the prisoners (the economic agents) to follow non-cooperative strategies. Repeated simulation studies have shown that cooperative strategies ensure a superior collective outcome to that of the dominant individualist strategies. The importance of cooperative action comes out more clearly in relation to the issues of distributive justice. For instance, as discussed above, the Rawlsian concept of 'justice as fairness' rests on the overarching idea of 'society as a fair system of cooperation among free and equal persons' [Rawls (1985)]. In such a societal context, economic agents are 'concerned' about the welfare of the other members of the society. It is through the cooperative action of such concerned individuals that 'just' social, economic and political structures can be created. This is particularly true of developing countries where structural change calls for cooperative action to resolve these problems in a satisfactory fashion.

Another relevant point in this context is that both the positivistic growth theories and the non-consequentialist moral theories typically emphasize such (implicit) values as 'opportunity', 'rights' and 'liberty', but say nothing about equality. Indeed, the importance of social and economic equality is played down in such economic and political theories. This is clearly unsatisfactory. If, according to the Rawlsian prescription, a just reordering of society requires cooperative strategies, equality—or, more accurately, movement towards this ideal—between the economic agents would be considered as important by those agents as their freedom. This aspect of the problem of structural change must be emphasized because a social consensus, based on a 'fair' system of distribution of rewards (and costs), is a necessary condition for political stability and economic progress in developing countries.

Do We Need Minimum Government?

We have already noted that the debate about the relative roles of the government and the market is as central to macro-economics as to development economics. This issue also appears in the moral-rights theories, both of which advocate 'minimum' government. Adam Smith pleaded for minimum government because the 'unintended consequences' of the selfish action of individuals will also largely, if not entirely, do the job that the government is supposed to, which is, to maximize social welfare. Following him, Friedman (1968), Lucas (1972), and other economists of the rational-expectationist school also seek to cut the government to a minimum, purely on a positivistic basis: the profit-maximizing economic agents, in reacting to government action, use up *all* the information that government has access to. As the element of surprise is thus eliminated from government action, adjustments to specific macro-economic policies—for instance, an increase in money supply—will occur spontaneously, and systematic, anticipated monetary or fiscal policies will have no effect on output or employment. Macro-economic management is, therefore, a pointless exercise—indeed, it is counter-productive. Buchanan (1986) shows that minimum government and an unfettered market follow from the moral argument that liberty has priority over all other values. Since only free markets, run by atomistic, profit-maximizing economic agents, preserve individual liberty, such arrangements are superior to any involuntary arrangements reached through the government. [See Chapters 3 and 4 for details.]

One of the most influential proponents of the 'minimum state' principle is Nozick. His moral argument for a minimal state is based on the principle of the priority of individual rights': 'Individuals have rights, and there are things no person or group may do to them (without violating their rights)'. He declares that 'the state may not use its coercive apparatus for the purpose of getting some citizens to aid others, or in order to prohibit activities to people for their own good or protection.' It is from this that Nozick's main assertion, 'moral values involve side constraints on action rather than merely being goal-directed', follows. Hence, it is morally wrong for the state to pursue universally accepted egalitarian goals, such as, the redistribution of income and wealth through any means whatsoever, including taxing the rich and distributing the proceeds among the poor. By the same token, the market is declared the best preserver of the individual's property rights because it avoids interfering with the individual's moral rights. State action is justified *only* if it is confined to the prevention of the violation of the individual's rights.

Nozick makes what is perhaps the strongest case for the market on moral grounds. He extends Locke's justification for a system of free markets based on the principle of mutual advantage. According to Locke, a market system, which allows free exchange and promotes division of labour, is the 'best alternative' to a hypothetical state of nature characterized by non-cooperation. Nozick goes further and maintains that, by virtue of its inherent quality of non-interference with the individual's rights, a market system is superior to any other system of cooperation even if this alternative system can be shown to be the mutually most advantageous! This is because, according to him, any other system of cooperation would interfere with the individual's rights.

Nozick's argument seeks to establish a case for limiting the role of the state in economic and social matters so that the existing curbs on individual freedom, even those prescribed for the individual's own good, are relaxed as far as possible. Taken literally, these arguments do not add up to much. Surprisingly, Nozick's argument rests on no systematic proof, heuristic or formal, in support of his advocacy of the unfettered rights of private property, the justification for which rests solely on procedures and rules framed by the state to regulate the processes of the acquisition and transfer of holdings. But, as Allen Buchanan (1985) notes, these arguments ignore the fact that the individual's voluntary exchanges in the market, though they may be morally unexceptionable in isolation, may be nevertheless cumulatively de-equalizing. Justice would, therefore, demand that some limitations be placed on the inequalities created as a result of the cumulative effects of individual exchanges.

Furthermore, it is scarcely desirable that a state create a given pattern of distribution of holdings by elaborate rules and procedures, which, according to Nozick, must be considered sacrosanct by all individuals and groups and by the state, and yet forswear the right to change this distribution pattern, even if the consequences turn out to be socially abominable. To maintain that the state can create an unfettered Frankenstein's monster through some legitimate procedure, and yet not be destroyed even when this creature spells destruction for the entire society, would be to confer an incredible degree of sanctity on rules and procedures per se. Nozick maintains that any state action to alleviate absolute or relative poverty, such as, by subsidizing the consumption of the poor and taxing the income and wealth of the rich, is illegitimate because it conflicts with the individual's (procedural) moral rights. This is stretching logic too far. Both commonsense and universally held mores and social norms contradict the view that the moral right of the individual against coercion is virtually unlimited. For these and other reasons, Nozick's theory has been criticised for being 'libertarianism without foundations', a criticism with which it is difficult to disagree.

Conjoining Ethics and Economics

I have been arguing that the ethical values of a society can be fruitfully integrated into the corpus of development theory and practice and that our ethico-moral values should be carefully chosen with reference to their social and economic consequences. To recapitulate, the point of departure of our inquiry is that the search for value-free or ethically neutral decision rules is both pointless and counter-productive. It is pointless because no such thing is possible. Even the Pareto-optimality rule is not entirely value-free; it involves a value judgement about preserving the status quo which is supposed to command unanimity. It is also counter-productive because a seeming unanimity about a given state of affairs is not necessarily a certain indicator of a universal endorsement.

For development economists, however, the problem does not end once economic problems have been analysed from a moral point of view. There is also the problem of choosing a set of moral values, which are beneficial to society, that is, values which ensure distributive justice, properly defined and within the context of a growing economy. Clearly, moral values which lead to the perpetuation of an unjust status quo in society cannot serve as an appropriate point of reference for economic analysis. But the strict non-consequentialist theories of moral 'rights', such as, Nozick's entitlement theory, fall in this category of 'immoral' morality, which is not acceptable to development economists. The Rawlsian maximin principle of justice, which focuses on maximizing the welfare of the worst-off individual(s) in society, is an example of the type of ethics that development economics should take as its 'reference point'. No meaningful theory can advocate the preservation of the status quo and still qualify as a valid development theory.

That being the case, we need a wider public-choice perspective which features ethics prominently. Unfortunately, value-free economics offers no help here because it considers moral rights only with regard to their consequences for the utility levels of economic agents. When it comes to the fulfilment of rights per se, these matters are normally considered legal questions of little intrinsic value for economic analysis. This is because such views directly contradict utilitarianism, on which much economic analysis is based. Harsanyi's equi-probability model of moral value-judgements, Hare's principle of 'universality', the Rawlsian conception of 'justice as fairness', the Suppe's grading principle, Sen's concept of 'capabilities', and many other such principles are not discussed here although they provide us with a wide array of formal models which explicitly feature ethical principles. Fundamentally, what these alternative choice-rules do is extend the somewhat restrictive concept of 'rationality', which positivist economics has come to accept and practise with a fanatical, unquestioning zeal, that self-interest-maximization is the only mover of the economic universe. Robbin's anti-ethicalism drove economics into this tight corner, but there is no need for it to remain squeezed there, with its face to the wall. At any rate, if ethical considerations do influence man's day-to-day behaviour, then it is not very sensible to assert that ethics do not matter. Universally accepted principles, namely, impartiality, universality, impersonality, which feature in the many decision rules reviewed briefly above, do affect man's behaviour. It will be sheer priggishness to insist that all such behaviour patterns are irrational because they are ethical.

It will be useful, therefore, to reconstruct development economics from the vantage-point of the social-choice theories which do not seek to rationalize the continuation of a socially undesirable status quo. This would open up new vistas for our discipline. Indeed, once the slavish attachment by economists to Pareto-optimality and by moral theorists to non-consequentialism are given up, development economists will be able to analyse important development problems more successfully. The problems of poverty and inequality and of assigning appropriate roles to the market and the government may be tackled in a logically consistent fashion, as they begin to employ both consequence-sensitive ethical philosophy and the positivistic arguments. What is required is to organize a marriage of ethics and economics to produce the desired results. Such a union will be mutually advantageous.

To maximize social welfare, behaviour that maximizes self-interest must be supplemented by a sympathy for others. The agents that maximize atomization must also appear in development models tempered by the exhilaration that comes from the position of other individuals in society, of being in someone else's shoes. Thus, moral rights, entitlements, liberty, and equality must feature in formal economic analysis to enhance its explanatory and predictive powers. This ought to be especially true of developing countries where most traditional institutional structures are unjust and need a complete overhauling. Efficiency-oriented criteria alone cannot help us to explain, let alone solve, the difficult problems of want, poverty, and human deprivation which darken the face of the developing countries.

Economic development is a painful process and it cannot be sustained without ensuring a modicum of equality among the citizens, without a just assignment of rights and duties, and without the active participation of the least-privileged in the society, whose welfare must be maximized, no matter what else is maximized.

NOTES

[1] It may be noted here that some important concepts in neo-classical economics have been borrowed from development economics—for instance, the Harris-Todaro market segmentation model [See Khan (1980)].

[2] Sen points out: 'Just as social choice may be based on individual preferences, the latter in their turn will depend on the nature of the society' [Sen (1970), p. 5].

[3] For a 'balanced' evaluation of Adam Smith's economic and philosophical viewpoints see, Skinner (1989).

[4] Robbins laid down that 'it does not seem logically possible to associate the two studies [ethics and economics] in any form but mere juxtaposition. Economics deals with ascertainable facts; ethics with valuation and obligations' [Robbins (1932)].

[5] This statement holds true only in the narrow Paretian sense.

[6] Empirical studies show that in the case of Japan—the most illustrious example of economic success based on a free-enterprise system—qualities like group loyalty, goodwill, sympathy and respect for others have played as much as decisive role as pure self-interest maximization behaviour. [Sen (1987)].

[7] Sen (1984) cites such a case: '...in guarding ownership rights against the demands of the hungry, the legal forces uphold entitlements, e.g., in the Bengal famine of 1943 the people who died in front of well-stocked food shops protected by the state were denied food because of lack of legal entitlement and not because of their entitlements being violated' (p. 458).

[8] However, see the recent work by Kreps (1990), who does assign a starring role to cooperative action.

6

Markets, Ethics, and Development Economics

In Chapters 3 and 5, I especially questioned the validity of
the arguments which seek to replace the view of an
economic universe beset by all-pervading market failures
with one of total government failure, as government intervention only spoils the utility/profit-maximizing effort by
giving rise to various activities of a rent-seeking type

[Krueger (1974)].[1] This chapter evaluates some of these arguments somewhat differently, in the light of the recent literature on the subject. It seeks to show that while considerations of static efficiency invite markets where they already exist, the dictates of equity and dynamic efficiency require government intervention, especially where markets do not exist due to external economies of various kinds. In the latter case, institutional constraints, created by the pattern of asset ownership and the mode of property relations, must be removed as a necessary condition to achieving both dynamic and static efficiency as well as equity in resource allocation. Thus, the standard corrective medicine, which is to get the prices right, does not work in all circumstances. Also, it follows that the cult of unqualified anti-*dirigisme,* and the expiatory rush to privatize, is ill-founded both in theory and practice—its frequent appeals to the 'first-best' rules of Pareto-optimality are misplaced.

THE STATE OF BLISS

The essence of the neo-classical cure for all ills is the adherence to the first-best rules of competitive efficiency—that is, to satisfy the equality between the domestic marginal substitution (in consumption) and the domestic marginal rate of transformation (in production), and that between the domestic rate of transformation and the foreign rate of transformation (through foreign trade), which, in turn, is equated to international prices. The implication is that competitive equilibrium will lead to an efficient allocation of domestic resources if the solution is secured through the market rather than through state intervention. Another remarkable result cited in support of market-oriented efficiency solutions is the two-way relationship between Pareto-optimality and competitive equilibrium. This relationship rests on the 'duality' property of an efficient resource allocation problem. Every maximum welfare problem has embedded in it a set of (shadow) prices, which correspond to optimal input prices—wages, rents, and interest rates. But for that to happen, a perfect, self-policing competition must obtain in all markets. This, in turn, requires that (contingent) markets exist for all situations, and that these markets 'clear' at all times. The resplendent world where all this happens is referred to as the 'state of bliss', secured by all-round convexities and multi-market Walrasian equilibria.

The Privatization Alchemy

Does it follow, then, that a policy of 'getting the (relative) prices right' will actually lead a real-world economy—made supplicant to price signals by large-scale privatization—to the state of bliss promised in the standard economics textbooks? Unbelievable as such a claim may seem, this is exactly what some economists seriously believe should, in fact, be the case. For instance, Lal (1983) thinks: 'The Utopian theoretical construct of perfect competition then becomes relevant as a reference point by which to judge the health of an economy, as well as the remedies suggested for its amelioration.' The proponents of the neo-classical political economy school consider the Pareto-optimal state as a counter-factual, distortion-free state, by reference to which the policy-induced (potential) waste of real resources can be measured.

This line of thinking is erroneous, both theoretically and empirically, as the following points show:

(a) It is generally forgotten that the existence of the Pareto-efficient configuration of product and input prices tells us only about rules which 'sustain' a bliss configuration that is *already in place.* As Bator (1958) points out, in the bliss situation 'we shall be concerned only with the prior problem whether a price-market system which finds itself at the maximum welfare point will or will not remain there.' It does not tell us *how to get there.* Thus, whether or not a policy of 'getting the prices right' will in fact land an economy with the 'wrong' prices in a state of bliss with the 'right' prices is not a sure thing—at least, not theoretically.

   (b) Obedience to the rules of allocative efficiency does not necessarily mean a shift from the government to the free market. This is because, to quote Bator (1958) again, 'the necessary conditions of decentralized price-profit calculations [hold] both in "laissez faire" and in a socialist setting of Lange-Lerner civil servants.' Also, the situations of failure of the basic duality property—that is, 'failure by existence,' 'failure by signal,' 'failure of incentive,' and 'failure by enforcement'—apply as much to 'laissez faire markets with genuine profit and satisfaction seekers' as to the 'decentralized efficiency of a Lange-Lerner type of [socialist] organisation scheme'. The only difference is that the conditions relating to a 'self-policing competitive' economy, characterized by very many producers in every market, will not be relevant in a socialist (market) economy. Whether the Pareto-optimal solution, which is supposed to maximize social welfare, is attained by the 'invisible hand' or calculated electronically by a computer does not matter at this level of discussion. All that is asserted is that 'an appropriate price system is associated with an efficient state' [Malinvaud (1969)], and that these prices are, strictly speaking, Lagrangean multipliers, which are formally equated with (shadow) profits, wages, and rents. However, note that these shadow prices may or may not equal market prices. Indeed, in all cases where external economies obtain, this equality will not hold—not even in theory.

131

The Newly Industrialized Countries

South Korea has been cited—for instance, by Little (1982)—as a showcase economy run according to the (Pareto-optimal) efficiency rules, and as one which has succeeded economically for that very reason. However, many competent observers of the South Korean miracle plead innocence of their Paretian proclivities.[2] Findlay (1988) points out that 'the experience of all NICs has been marked not only by a strong reliance on world market forces, but also by very far-reaching and pervasive intervention and control in all segments of the economy.' Even the export bias displayed by South Korea (and also by Brazil) can hardly be cited as a model of liberalism; instead, the practice of dumping through market segmentation—by making the domestic consumer pay significantly more for the same product than the foreign consumer—is more an example of mercantilism than of trade liberalism. As for the argument that this latter-day strong export bias in some sense may have cancelled the early equally strong import-substitution bias, thus creating conditions approaching the first-best state of bliss promised by Pareto-optimality, is really stretching Vilfredo Pareto's meaning a little too far.[3]

According to Bardhan (1988):

> it is by now well-known that the favourite neo-classical showcase of South Korea is not predominantly one of market liberalism but of aggressive and judiciously selective state intervention. The Korean state has heavily used the illiberal compliance mechanism of selective command and administrative discretion, restricting imports for industrial promotion, disciplining the private sector through control over domestic credit and foreign exchange and underwriting of foreign borrowing, and public enterprises leading the way in many areas.

In other words, South Korea, like Pakistan, India, and

other developing countries has rebelled against the first-best rules of market efficiency (and Pareto-optimality) in every possible way, with state intervention being used in its qualitative as well as quantitative manifestations. Of course, one could still persist with the anti-*dirigiste* thesis and maintain that 'it is not outlandish to believe that South Korea, especially, would have done even better if its government had intervened less...' [Crook (1989)]. But this is more an assertion of *faith*, based on a metaphysical belief in the superiority of free markets, rather than a scientific statement.

The (logical) falsity of making generalizations about the benefits of privatization from the South Korean case and those of the others in the group of NICs—even assuming that this is what the NICs actually have done—becomes obvious by considering the case of Chile, which pushed privatization to its limits but has not done very well economically. Yotopoulos (1989) has observed that privatization, especially of capital markets, has not led to higher levels of saving and investment. Indeed, gross fixed capital investment during 1974-1982 was only 15 per cent of the GDP as compared with 21 per cent of the GDP during the 1960s, when the privatization fever had not yet taken hold of Chile. The so-called democratization of the ownership of national assets, or making ownership more broad-based, also did not come about. Indeed, the concentration of economic power in major banking groups increased. To add insult to injury, industrial efficiency did not improve either. Indeed, industrial profitability declined during the period of fervent privatization.

Do Markets Always Deliver?

As we noted, a regime of competitive efficiency implies a set of shadow prices—which have all the analytical characteristics of profit, wages, and rent. If these prices are set equal to each factor's marginal (revenue) product, then, by Euler's

Theorem, total output will be exactly apportioned among the factors of production—in cases where the production function is linear and homogeneous of degree 'one' (constant returns to scale). As no (Marxian) surplus output is left over, no exploitation of labour (or capital) is ever possible— mathematically, that is. Also, as labour markets eventually clear, no possibility of (involuntary) unemployment emerges when bliss configurations of input and output (shadow) prices prevail.

Another related train of thought is as follows: the fundamental theorem of welfare economics asserts not only that every perfectly competitive equilibrium is Pareto-optimal, but also that, for some distribution of endowments to be determined, every Pareto-optimal state is also a perfectly competitive equilibrium. The second part of the theorem is important: does the market ensure that the initial distribution of endowments among the economic agents is equitable? And how does it do it, if at all it does so? The neo-classical answer is that if lump sum or some other non-distortionary transfers *could* be made by the gainers to the losers from a change, and if there were still some left-over, then the change in question is unequivocally efficient. Even though it is not always explicitly asserted, such a state is by the same token regarded as equitable.

Another assurance about the alleged equity of the state of bliss comes from economists like Coase (1960), Buchanan and Stubblebine (1962), and others, who show that the Pigovian market failure to (re)distribute property rights takes place not because of some inherent defect of the market mechanism, but because such rights are not adequately defined. Hence, it is shown that, in a game-theoretic framework, the outcome of a bargaining process about property rights will be Pareto-optimal and efficient, if property rights are properly defined and freely exchanged. The Pareto-optimal situation, according to this line of thinking, will be attained by moving onto a new 'contract curve' through bilateral trading between parties.

Let us examine these arguments. First, as Robinson (1979) points out, the Marxian thesis about the exploitation of labour by the capitalists—that profits and the competitive rate of profits are directly linked with 'surplus value'—is in no way vitiated by the neo-classical fiction about distributing total output according to the marginal productivity theory, which does not make a clear distinction between the sources of income and the factors of production. As to the Hicksian costless lump sum 'payments' by potential gainers to potential losers from a change, it may be noted that such lump sum transfers that 'could be made' are never in fact made—in the ascetic tradition of welfare economics! But this is neither here nor there. If the welfare of those who lose because of the change is to be actually increased, then such transfers should actually be made.[4]

Second, it has been shown—for example, by Bowles (1985)—that market equilibrium is characterized by (involuntary) unemployment because the wage rate actually paid by the employer exceeds the market-clearing wage. This may happen in the rural areas to avoid labour shortages in the peak season [Bardhan (1988)], and in the urban areas to economise on-the-job training costs [Shapiro and Stiglitz (1984)]. Malinvaud (1984) shows that most observed unemployment is of the involuntary (disequilibrium) variety, mainly because of the non-existence of a market-clearing wage rate. He, therefore, concludes that, in general, 'permanent market clearing is an untenable hypothesis'. Also, in the Harris-Todaro model, the equality of (expected) wages fails to clear the (urban) labour market, so that equilibrium in a segmented labour market co-exists with urban unemployment, which is fed by continuing rural-urban migration [Khan (1987a)].

Third, for market efficiency to lead to an equitable redistribution of the existing *legally sanctioned* private property rights, the transaction costs are assumed to be zero. But, since bargaining is a costly and time-consuming affair, this assumption will be seldom met. With positive transaction costs—especially those incurred to keep out the free-riders, the familiar externality scenario will arise, which the market will fail to cure [Furubotn and Pejovich (1972)]. A more fundamental point is that, in the Coase (1960)–Buchanan (1962) type of solution, it is essential that each individual makes available information about his initial endowments to provide a basis for choice among various Pareto-optimum states—to choose the 'optimum optimorum'. But such information is hardly ever truthfully revealed, without violating the ground rules of a decentralized regime of free markets. One of these ground rules is that the individual utility functions are not known to each other, and that there is no mechanism available to the market to make any individual reveal the information about his utility (production) functions to another individual. That being the case, Arrow (1979) shows that 'a procedure which would achieve a Pareto-efficient allocation if each agent knew the other's utility function will have a positive probability of falling short of efficiency if this knowledge is absent.' And since such knowledge is indeed absent, it follows that a Pareto-efficient solution secured through the bargaining process will not necessarily be efficient!

This last result is also relevant for examining the question of private property rights—whether the market process, by itself, will lead, á la Coase, to an equitable distribution of (initial) property rights.[5] Arrow (1979) shows that such an outcome depends crucially on the (unstated) assumption that the players in a cooperative game 'know every other player's pay-off (utility, profit, whatever) as a function of the strategies played'. But, as shown above, the existence of such a knowledge runs contrary to the rules of the competitive markets.

Therefore, it follows that the state of bliss of the economics textbook may not even be approximated, let alone actually achieved, in the real world for more than one reason: the lump sum transfers from the gainers to the losers from a change are not actually made; (involuntary) unemployment co-exists with market equilibrium; and an equitable redistribution of property and asset holdings cannot be brought about by the market.

The 'Invisible Foot'

We have already noted that, of late, there have been many statements about the innate tendency to fail government. By contrast, new-fangled 'neo-classical political economy,' using strictly positivistic reasoning, asserts that all-pervading government interventions in the economic processes have led to the creation of the rent-seeking activity [Krueger (1974)] and to directly unproductive profit-seeking (DUP) activities [Bhagwati (1982)], thereby leading to a wastage of real resources. Brock and Magee (1984) have used the metaphor of an (inefficient) 'Invisible Foot' which tramples all over the (efficient) 'Invisible Hand'. This odd vision is but another name for government, which is seen as preventing the forces of free competition from maximizing social welfare through the (unproductive) activities of the profit-seekers— the 'profits' or rents which can be eliminated by restoring the world to the bliss of perfect competition.

This line of thought assumes market processes to be without cost in terms of providing the necessary information for making production decisions and, consequently, that a shift from the market to the government imposes an avoidable dead-weight loss on the economy. This is not a point of much logical worth because, as North (1984) points out, 'there is no meaningful standard of Pareto-efficiency possible, since one cannot specify a least-cost structure of government for any given level of output.' Furthermore, such arguments also implicitly equate competitive efficiency (and Pareto-optimality) with the efficiency of the (private) market in the real world. As we have seen, this position is hard to defend, especially because the information provided by the market is also costly.

Becker (1983) believes that government probably could help achieve the social optimum but will not do so, because governments represent and serve vested interests. This may be too narrow and cynical a view of government. Notwithstanding their penchant for underhand politicking, governments do have a 'conception of national interest' [Miliband (1983)]. Furthermore, such cynical neo-classical views of the state do not explain how, over time, different interventionist states become development states in some cases though not in others. The explanation seems to lie in the ability of the development states to insulate economic management from wasteful rent-seeking activities. Even in cases where such insulation is not achieved, it would be naive to suggest that leaving the process to the market would solve all problems because, as Bardhan (1988) notes, 'the very reasons why insulation is infeasible are often also the ones which will make first-best policies inoperative, and in the absence of lump sum redistribution, a policy of relative inaction may be distributionally unacceptable.'

The fact of the matter is that inherent (generalized) government failure cannot be asserted in the same sense as the Marshall-Pigou type of (selective) market failure. partly because government policies, for better or worse, set the parameters within which the market functions—perhaps efficiently. The utility-maximizing calculus, based only on the consumption of the (private) goods by the individual, cannot take him far without the availability of public goods and without the constitutional guarantees of the free consumption of the private goods, both of which are provided by the state. At any rate, the process of growth, and the attendant (painful) structural adjustment required for this process to continue unhindered, cannot be propelled by the utility/profit-maximizing economic agents alone. A sovereign state must initiate 'policy action and institutions are required [to minimize] the costs of, and resistance to, the structural shifts implicit in, and required for, a high rate of growth' [Kuznets (1971)].

FREE MARKETS AND INDIVIDUAL FREEDOM

In recommending that developing economies adopt free markets to achieve efficiency (and growth), the neo-classical economists are really advocating the adoption of the doctrine of Pareto-optimality by development economics. According to them, the observance of this rule is 'desirable' because it is allegedly 'fair' and reflects unanimity, since the rule requires that the preferences held universally in a society should be reflected in any scheme of social judgement. It is also liberal, because it preserves liberty, which is the basic value to be cherished by all civilized societies. Thus, the passion for Pareto-optimality is not only held to be rational, but it is also regarded as the only civilized option. Let us examine these claims a little more carefully.

Does Pareto-optimality preserve individual liberty? The answer is firmly in the negative. Sen (1970) shows the incompatibility of the Pareto principle, both in its strong and weak forms, with even a rudimentary kind of individual liberty. Assuming as 'unrestricted domain' (U), Pareto-optimality (P), and 'Liberalism' (L), Sen demonstrates that 'there is no social decision function that can simultaneously satisfy U, P, and L.' Here liberalism—or more accurately, libertarianism—is defined in a very elementary sense of recognizing each individual's privilege to have a minimum of what Hayek (1960) calls every individual's 'protected sphere'. In other words, each individual should have the freedom to make 'at least one social choice, for example, having his own walls painted pink rather than white, other things remaining the same for him and the rest of the society.' The implication of Sen's Impossibility Theorem, which modifies Arrow's celebrated Impossibility Theorem, is quite disturbing: it shows that Pareto-optimality, given the assumption U—that is, every logically possible set of individual ordering is included in the domain of the collective-choice rule—cannot be combined with even a minimum dose of liberalism. Hence, if Pareto-optimality is followed to its logical (bitter) end, then 'society cannot let more than one individual be free to read what they like, sleep the way they prefer, dress as they care to, etc., irrespective of the preferences of others in the community.' Surely, these consequences are 'most illiberal.'[6] It may seem, therefore, that even to be able to breathe freely one may have no option but to free oneself from the smothering embrace of Pareto-optimality!

Is the Pareto-optimality rule 'fair'? Alas, the answer is again in the negative, and for the following reasons:

(a) The Pareto-optimality rule is distributionally neutral.[7] Yes, but in the weird sense that, from the society's point of view, the equal and extremely unequal outcomes are equally preferable! It should be obvious that, with this definition of neutrality, one cannot meaningfully make judgements about the problems of income distribution.

(b) The Pareto-optimality rule is blind to whether a person is rich or poor. This follows from the utilitarian (indeed, welfarist) character of Pareto-optimality. As is well known, Pareto-optimality—indeed (new) Welfare Economics—regards social welfare as an increasing function of personal utility levels alone. It denies admission rights once and for all to any type of non-utility information, that individual utilities are non-comparable, and that individual utilities are ranked ordinally, not cardinally. But these very characteristics incapacitate the Pareto rule *to differentiate the rich from the poor,* even in broad daylight.[8]

It follows from *(a)* and *(b)* above that the Pareto rule precludes economists, especially development economists, paying any attention whatsoever to the problems of liberty, income equality, and poverty—perhaps so that they may specialize completely on efficiency! If, as according to Lewis (1984), development economics is a study of the economic structure and behaviour of poor countries, to follow Pareto-optimality alone in making a collective choice is indeed a prescription for social disaster.

ON BEING EQUAL

Another characteristic of Pareto-optimality is its proclaimed 'value-free' character, in line with the stand taken by (neo-classical) economists against relying on normative judgements for making social decisions [Robbins (1932)]. But is it really so? In so far as the Pareto rule relies on unanimity about certain value judgements—for example, not disturbing the status quo with respect to income distribution—this state of affairs is by no means without a value judgement and it is certainly not value-free. Be that as it may, the fact is that such a stance disqualifies Pareto-optimality as the bedrock of development economics, which aims explicitly at socio-economic change—indeed, at a structural transformation of poor societies into well-to-do societies.

How Equal is Equality?

In the poor countries, a central value judgement, indeed an ethical judgement, must be made: it is desirable to guide the developing economies towards greater equality of distribution of income and wealth between different classes of the society, especially between the rich and the poor. An explicit commitment to some such ideal is essential to ensure (voluntary) universal participation by all classes of society in the process of economic development, so that both the costs and the benefits of social change are equitably shared. If Pareto-optimality cannot see the difference between the rich and the poor, it reveals its own shortcomings. We then need some other social choice rule that does 'see' this vital difference.

Let it be noted that equality between the rich and the poor does not mean *complete* equality. Indeed, no one, including Karl Marx, has ever suggested this. All that equality is meant to imply is that economic processes are directed to minimize, not necessarily to eliminate, the inter-class distributional differences as far as is economically and socially permissible. A relevant consideration in this context is the Rawlsian maxim: 'inequalities are arbitrary unless it is reasonable to expect that they will work out for everyone's advantage, and provided only the position and offices to which they attach, or from which they may be gained, are open to all' [Rawls (1971)]. According to this rule, the creation and the existence of income inequalities may be ethically justifiable provided only that the basic institutions of the society are also restructured in such a manner that the new economic and social possibilities opened up by economic progress are equally accessible to the various classes of society.

The goal of equality, in fact, has been pursued by economists explicitly since the days of Bentham. But equality itself has been defined differently by various schools of thought. One can distinguish four main types of equality:

142

there is the 'utilitarian equality,' the 'total utility equality,' the 'Rawlsian equality,' and the 'basic capability equality.'[9] Of these, the first two types of equalities are scarcely realizable. Utilitarian equality requires the equality of the marginal utility of everyone. But to restrict the equalization process to the utility space alone is really to prevent it from doing any good to the individual or the society. As noted above, if looking at different persons' marginal utilities alone does not let the observer see the difference between the rich and the poor— mainly because of the exclusion of interpersonal comparisons— then not much social change can come about by following this principle. In particular, once we come to the distribution of utilities, utilitarianism offers no comfort to the poor; for even the smallest gain in the total utility sum would over-balance the worst type of distributional inequality on this scale. This problem can be avoided if it is assumed that everyone has the same utility function. But that is really to trivialize the problem of inequality—which is marked by the fact that different persons' utility functions are not the same. The equalization of total utility is a more helpful guide— particularly, its leximin version, according to which the goodness of a state is judged by the utility level of the worst-off individual. But that, too, is unsatisfactory because, by definition, it ignores the intensity of the person's needs and is also insensitive to the magnitude of the potential utility gains and losses.

The main problem with both these types of equality is their insistence on using the utility information only as an index of individual and social welfares. This exclusive insistence on utility information, marginal or total, can lead to a situation in which more income is given to the less needy, simply because he is the hard-to-please type, and the poor person, who is easily satisfied even with small mercies, will have less income! But equally interesting information about a person's welfare is of the non-utility type—for instance, the possession of certain types of goods, or the possession of certain capabilities to do some basic things essential for man's survival. Accordingly, discussed below are the remaining two types of equality which explicitly use such non-utility information: (a) *Rawlsian equality* and *(b) Sen's basic capability equality.*

(a) Rawlsian Equality: As explained several times in these pages, the central thrust of the Rawlsian conception of equality is its focus on bringing about institutional changes, such as to 'make the worst-off best-off'—that is, such action as would raise the welfare level of the worst-off individual in tne society as far as it is possible to [Rawls (1971)]. This is the so-called Rawlsian Difference Principle. Rejecting utility as the basis of individual welfare, Rawls, instead, defines welfare in terms of a bundle of 'primary goods', which are defined as 'things that every rational man is presumed to want'. These things include 'rights, liberties and opportunities, income and wealth, and the social bases of self-respect'. Institutional arrangements which guarantee the access of the worst-off individuals to these primary goods are both efficient and equal. The Difference Principle is held to be 'just' because it is chosen 'fairly' in the 'original position', which denotes a (mental) experiment of passing through a 'veil of ignorance' to make impartial decisions about the structure of the society. Unlike the utilitarian principle, Rawls allows interpersonal comparisons to judge the fairness of the distribution of primary goods among individuals.

There are many problems with this principle of equality also, especially because the needs (for primary goods) of a disadvantaged person—say a cripple or a sick person—do not get registered at all in the Rawlsian calculus, and there are other technical points that need not be recounted here. But the emphasis of Rawlsian equality on institutional change, on the welfare of the least-privileged, on 'justice as fairness', and on the availability of 'primary goods' to all without discrimination of any kind are elements which should find an explicit expression in any sensible model of development economics.

(b) *Basic Capability Equality.* Sen (1984) goes a step beyond the Rawlsian emphasis on equality with respect to primary goods—towards 'what goods do to human beings'. Equality is insisted on with respect to such capabilities. Shifting attention from goods to capabilities has the advantage of explicitly taking into account the differences in people's 'needs' and requirements—something that the Rawlsian and the utilitarian concepts of equality fail to do. Such differences, arising from the conversion of goods into capabilities, are allowed in Sen's concept of equality, as also the differences arising from the nature of different societies. 'The notion of the equality of basic capability is a very general one, but any applications of it must be culture-dependent, especially in the weighting of different capabilities.'

EFFICIENCY AND JUSTICE

The brief survey of the various concepts of equality in the last section underscores four basic points which are of a fundamental importance for development economics. *First,* normative judgements are routinely made when it comes to the problems of personal or social welfare. *Second,* these normative judgements are based on an ethical perception of human beings who not only are free but are also seen as free—in being equally entitled to the most extensive basic amenities and liberties that a society has to offer. *Third,* there is the emphasis on changing the status quo and doing positive things to change the basic structure of the society mainly by producing greater equality among different human beings. *Fourth*, the emphasis is on justice and fairness as well as on efficiency. It is not one thing to the exclusion of the other. All these points should be taken care of in our perception of the process of economic development, which should aim both at growth and equitable distribution of the fruits of economic progress—things that a blind adherence to the Pareto rule would not enable us to see, much less do.

A guide-book up the road of economic progress, which contains directions only about efficiency and nothing of substance about equity, cannot be recommended for development economics. Once the development process is looked at, á la Rawls, as one that requires a rearrangement of the basic structure of the society which is 'fair' and 'just'—that which focuses on the needs of the least-privileged in the society—the standard prescription of 'getting the prices right' and then letting the free market take its course is, by and large, wrong-headed. An exclusive reliance on the market mechanism cannot bring about a structural transformation—especially in matters of redistributing private property rights, for the simple reason that it can neither initiate the growth process nor can it, by itself, adjust to a clash of vested interests.

The challenge facing development economics is not one of devising docking strategies to join the mother-ship of neoclassical economics, nor is it one of declaring independence from neoclassical economics. What is required is the evolution of a synthetic view of economic process requiring both macro and micro insights—one which is based on a wider set of social choice theories not restricted to Pareto-optimality. Social action should be made sensitive to the intensity of individual preferences, and not just to individual preferences; interpersonal comparisons of the welfare should be allowed to comprehend the differences in the social station of different individuals; and due account should be taken of the nature of the societal structure with reference to the social choices made.

NOTES

[1]According to these arguments, the development experience of the last four decades—especially of the 'Gang of Four', namely South Korea, Singapore, Taiwan, and Hong Kong—is seen as supporting this vision. Citing the contrast between free markets and centrally-planned economies, and the recent disavowal of the socialist economic philosophy by Eastern Europe, Haberler concludes: 'I still maintain my early belief in the validity of classical or neoclassical theory and in the superiority of relying largely on competitive markets and private enterprise' [Haberler (1988)]. In the same vein, the ultra-conservative *Economist* (London) declares: 'After three decades the experience of these countries [shows that] history chooses the invisible hand' [Crook (1989)]. Thus, it is alleged that development economics, born of the idea of an interventionist government is a discredited discipline.

[2]See, Jones and Sakong (1980), and Pack and Westphal (1986).

[3]Findlay (1988) calls such appeals 'Pareto-optimality by inadvertence'.

[4]Graaff (1989) makes the same point: 'What does it help to say that, although several men will starve, the cost to the society is low, because they *could* be given sufficient food to prevent their starving?'

[5]This result, due to Coase, is often referred to as the Say's Law of Welfare Economics [Calabresi (1968)].

[6]Sen (1970) warns: 'If someone takes the Pareto principle seriously, as economists seem to do, then he has to face the problem of consistency in cherishing liberal values, even very mild ones.'

[7]Let us understand clearly the meaning of 'neutrality.' Following Sen (1985), suppose there are two states x and y. The neutrality property demands that if (x, y) is replaced by (a, b) in everyone's preference ordering, then we must do the same in social ordering as well. In other words, for making a social choice it does not matter what the nature of x, y, a, b is; all that matters is the existence of individual perferences over these states. The problem is posed in the following manner: suppose x = equal division of cake, and y = nothing for person 1 and equal division for persons 2 and 3.

Development Economics

According to the neutrality property, it does not matter if x, y are replaced by a, b. Let a = nothing for 2 and 3 and all for 1; and b = equal division. Neutrality demands that x is socially preferred to y, if and only if a is socially preferred to b.

[8]To see this clearly, it would be best to quote from Sen (1979):

> Can we identify the rich through the observation that they have more utility than the poor? Not in the Arrow framework, since interpersonal comparisons are not admitted. Perhaps as those with a lower marginal utility of income? No, of course not, since that will go against *both* non-comparability and ordinalism. Can we then distinguish the rich as those who happen to have more income, or more consumer goods (nothing about utility need be said), and bring this recognition to bear in social judgements? No, not that either, since this will go against welfarism (and against strict ranking-welfarism), since this discrimination has to be based on non-utility information.

[9]This discussion draws largely on Sen (1983*a*).

7

A Paradigmatic View of Development Economics

In this final chapter, I intend to highlight the paradigmatic character of development economics and to emphasize its deeply ethical nature and its vision of a mixed economy. These aspects of our discipline have been examined, in varying degrees, in the preceding chapters, but there are still some outstanding issues that need greater elaboration to both clarify further and conclude the discussion. Even at the risk of some repetition, we begin by looking at the roots of the discipline to see how it has grown over time and what needs to be done to ensure its (steady-state) growth as a discipline in its own right.

THE ROOTS

The lineage of development economics has been variously described. Sen (1988) considers William Petty to be 'certainly' the 'founder of development economics' because of his earthshaking observation that 'the French grow too fast'! Lewis's (1988) archaeological explorations find the subject buried in the eighteenth-century writings of Hume, Cantillon, Smith and Wallace, among others. Indeed, according to him, the lineage of our discipline goes further back in time: 'The theory of economic development established itself in Britain in the century and a half running from 1650 to Adam Smith's *The Wealth of Nations* (1776)', and many of the concepts of modern development economics were already in currency in those days.[1] All this makes interesting reading but is not very useful in getting a hold on the paradigmatic character of development economics—that it represents a genuine revolution in the realm of economic knowledge. Between the occasional concern among the classical economists about economic development in the days of yore and the many-sided, perennial intellectual activity of development economics with a distinctive research programme of its own in the modern times, there is only a tenuous link.

The fact of the matter is that one does not have to go back more than fifty years or so to see the new discipline still in its infancy. Its foundations were all but laid between Rosenstein-Rodan's 'big-push' conjecture (1943) and Lewis's celebrated two-sector model (1954), based on the dual concepts of an unlimited supply of labour in the rural sector and a capitalist urban sector. In between, we had Prebisch's (1950)-Singer's (1950) export pessimism; Gerschenkron's 'pioneers-latecomers' syndrome (1962); Nurkse's 'balanced-growth' hypothesis (1953); and Mahalanobis's heavy-industry advocacy (1953). And a little later comes Hirschman's (1958) 'unbalanced growth' hypothesis. In these contributions we have the first glimpses of a new 'paradigm', with economic *development* and not *just* efficient *growth* as its central theme. Such a concern with the growth of the key inputs (which are labour and capital) over time, rather than with their efficient use in a static economic framework, was dictated by conditions of extreme resource scarcity in the 'initial conditions'.

According to these formulations, the process of economic development is initiated and then sustained along the growth path by continuous capital (saving) accumulation in the capitalist sector, and helped by a perfectly elastic (or un-limited) supply of labour in the rural sector—resembling the Marxian reserve army of labour. All investment (saving) is made by the capitalists out of their profits. Hence, the rate of growth in a dynamic equilibrium is determined by the profit rate multiplied by the capitalist's saving. The distribution of income is likely to worsen, at least initially. The process of growth in the framework of a closed economy, or in one nearly closed by excessive export-elasticity pessimism, would be a 'balanced' one in case of elastic supplies of the key industrial inputs, making a maximum use of the horizontal and vertical interdependencies between sectors. However, it would be 'unbalanced' if investment resources were assumed to be fixed with the explicit aim of attaining some kind of a dynamic balance—or of 'exploiting dynamic external economies' [Scitovsky (1954)]—but would happen only by suffering, in the interregnum, an appropriate dose of 'creative tensions'.

This is borne out by the experience of the 'pioneers' (the Europeans) who, according to Rostow (1956), Ohlin (1959) and Gerschenkron (1962), grew by taking advantage of vertical interdependencies between sectors. The 'latecomers' can grow even faster than the pioneers by learning from the latter's experience and by drawing upon their 'book of blueprints' of technical knowledge *free of cost*. The state may have to intervene when the factor prices do not reflect the opportunity costs, when sizeable external economies exist, or when there are large complementarities between the sectors. The less the opportunities of profitable international exchange, the more important will be these factors.

Development policy and, to some extent, development theory drew freely on the Keynesian (paradigmatic) Revolution and its immediate successor, the Harrod-Domar model. From the former, development economics also derived the courage to declare independence—or, more accurately, autonomy—from mainstream classical economics. What is more, some of the new discipline's intellectual armoury consisted of concepts which were directly inspired by the Keynesian Revolution—for instance, the concept of 'rural underemployment', a first cousin of the Keynesian unemployment equilibrium and the vision of a mixed economy, with the state playing a dominant role to correct the strategic macro-economic imbalances that the market cannot do much about. However, cross-fertilization of ideas was the most intense with the Harrod-Domar model, from where development economics has derived its central concepts— the national savings rate (s), the capital-output ratio (v), and the growth of the labour force (n), *without* being enamoured of the foibles of steady-state growth paths. Not being excessively concerned about the highly restrictive assumptions on which the Harrod-Domar model was based, development economists were more interested in the model's predictions.[2] These predictions relate to the key role played by the growth of labour supply, which sets the upper limit on the sustainable growth rate of output, and to the basic result that, given a technologically fixed capital/output ratio and growth rate of employment, the economy can be made to grow twice as fast only if the savings rate is twice as high. (Note that here 'capital' is exclusively *physical* capital.)

THE DEFECT OF HERITAGE

Let us now note some of the weaknesses—indeed, the disabilities—of the development paradigm that has just been described. First, a basic weakness relates to the centrality of the savings rate in the process of growth—an aspect of the Harrod-Domar model that development economists accepted uncritically. It was not clearly understood that increasing the *ex ante* savings rate will not automatically increase the *ex post* savings rate unless specific steps are taken to raise the *ex ante* investment rate as well. The correct proposition that a higher rate of growth of savings will permit the economy to grow at a higher rate *for some time* was sometimes confused with the wrong statement that a higher growth of savings is required to achieve a *permanent* increase in the rate of output.[3]

Second, the crucial role of the technological process, first highlighted by Schumpeter (1934), in generating a sufficiently high (*ex ante*) rate of investment to raise output on a permanent, rather than on a transitory, basis was not clearly reflected in development models. Looking back, this appears. to be a rather surprising omission because Solow's classic article (1957) showed clearly whatever is involved in correcting the built-in instability of the Harrod-Domar model, according to which all its three elements (n, v, s) are given constants for various reasons: the trick is to let the capital/output ratio vary due to technological change. There is a yet deeper reason why technological change must be brought into the picture: without it, the per capita income will at best grow at a *constant* rate, along the steady-state growth path. But this is not what development economics is concerned about; instead, it is concerned primarily with the ways and means of *raising* the per capita income (output) over time.

Third, the human factor—especially education—was not assigned the importance it deserved in these models. This is strange, because Solow had shown clearly that about seven-tenths of the increase in gross output per hour of work in the U.S. between 1909 and 1945 was due to 'technological progress in the broadest sense'. What it means is that the contributions of physical capital and labour were considerably less important than one would normally have thought—to the chagrin of both Lewis and Marx! Later, Denison [(1967), (1985)] showed in his growth-accounting framework that a full 30 per cent of the per capita growth of output between 1929 and 1982 was accounted for by education per worker, while 64 per cent of it was explained by the advance in knowledge.

Fourth, Lewis's two-sector model led to a frame of thinking in which the growth potentialities of the agricultural sector were grossly underestimated. This is damaging because, as Johnston-Mellor (1961) show clearly, 'economic development is characterized by a substantial increase in the demand for agricultural products, and failure to expand food supplies in pace with the growth of demand can seriously impede economic growth.' This is so because 'if food supplies fail to expand in pace with the growth of demand, the result is likely to be a substantial rise in food prices, leading to political discontent and pressure on wage rates with adverse effects on industrial profits, investment, and economic growth.' Kalecki (1971) echoed the same theme: the process of development is constrained by the availability of capital; but investment is determined not only by savings but also by the supply of wage goods, which are typically supplied by the agricultural sector. There is another reason, again recognized by Mellor-Johnston (1984), why the development of agriculture is crucial: it relates to the role of varying the capital/output-ratio to maximize output in terms of the required capital inputs—an echo of Solow. Recognizing that 'extremely low capital/labour-ratio in the dominant rural sector is at the heart of the development problem', it would clearly be desirable to 'spread' the scarce capital resource between the low capital/labour-ratio agriculture sector and the relatively higher capital/labour-ratio industrial sector.

Fifth, as we noted in Chapter 1, the original development paradigm is also inadequate because of its 'bloody-mindedness' with respect to the distributional aspect of growth.[4] Indeed, in Lewis's two-sector model with unlimited supplies of labour, economic growth is a function solely of the profit rate: 'the central fact of economic development is that the distribution of income is altered in favour of the saving class' [Lewis (1954)]. Thus, in this model, the distribution path is completely determined by the rate of economic growth, with the wage-earners losing out to the capitalists, and a rise, for whatever reason, in the real wage rate signals a weakening of the growth impulse. In the Fei-Ranis model (1963), a less fatalistic scenario is presented: once all surplus labour has migrated and the urban wage starts to rise, the wage-earners will find their lots improved. Thus, in the growth process no one income group loses out *absolutely*. But, somehow, Lewis's lesson was absorbed by the first generation of development economists. [For instance, Galenson and Leibenstein (1955), and Kaldor (1955).]

In this respect, one should think that development economists were marching with the spirit of the times. For instance, according to the so-called classical savings function, used by the neo-Keynesians, such as Robinson (1979), the rate of growth of income is simply a function of the savings of the profit-earners multiplied by the profit rate. The empirical studies done by Kuznets (1955) lent respectability to this view by reference to the forces of history, according to which income inequity tends to increase in the initial stages as income rises—following an inverted 'U' pattern, and income inequalities tend to be bigger in the poor countries than in the rich countries. That may be so, but the fact that growth has been accompanied by income inequality does not mean that no steps can or ought to be taken to remedy this. It should, at least, be possible to state unambiguously that growth combined with a more equitable distribution is superior to growth combined with a less equitable distribution. The founding fathers of development economics did not give distributional matters the serious thought they deserved—an omission that would cost many of these countries dearly in terms of the loss of potential output.[5]

MAKING A VIRTUE OF A DEFECT

A somewhat defective heritage is better than no heritage at all; indeed, given a lively on-going intellectual debate, such 'defects' lead to a better—but never a perfect—paradigm. Hirschman (1981b) thought that development economics was a 'done thing' because it did not respond creatively to the many challenges it faced both from the Left and the Right. But a spate of sympathetic review-articles and full-length books have appeared at regular intervals since then.[6] With such credentials and such vitality, development economics can be hardly faulted for intellectual moribundity. In fact, its response to the changing realities of life in the developing countries, and to the new theoretical advances made in mainstream economics, has been both positive and creative.

The 'Meaning' of Development

In the light of development experience, a large body of literature has appeared focusing on a more comprehensive indicator of social welfare than the GNP. Morris (1979) suggested a Physical Quality Index (PQLI), including life expectancy, infant mortality, and literacy as components. The problem here is that life expectancy and infant mortality are significantly correlated. The basic-needs approach [Streeten et al. (1981)], which enjoyed the blessings of the World Bank, also tried to provide an answer. Even though somewhat 'open-ended' with respect to its theoretical underpinnings, it did correctly highlight the need for making a greater provision for the social sectors. Sen's (1981) study of famines has led him to look at the development process as a matter of 'entitlements' and 'capabilities' [Sen (1984)] and, ultimately, of enlarging people's choices; and to concentrate on the means (namely, growth) instead of the ends (such as, longevity, literacy, freedom).

A similar formulation appears in a recent UNDP report (1990), where the concept of human development is introduced to encompass 'the production and distribution of commodities and the expansion and use of human capabilities'. An HDI (Human Development Index), taking account of longevity, knowledge, and basic income, replaces the GNP as an indicator of economic *development*—as distinct from economic *growth*. The first two elements of this index measure the formation of human capabilities, while the third one serves as a proxy variable for the use of these capabilities. There are some obvious problems with this approach, as there are with the way the HDI is constructed. First, to focus on the ends rather than the means of development may lead to confusion, theoretically and practically, since the ends are not uniquely related to the means—so that specifying the former does not unambiguously fix the latter. It is, thus, a question-begging proposition. Second, the suggestion that the GDP be adjusted by the relevant Gini Coefficient to yield a more welfare-oriented (cross-country) ranking is certainly well-taken, but it is problematic when the Lorenz Curves intersect over the relevant range. However, even when they do not intersect, the welfare ranking is not invariant with respect to the type of the inequality measure used.[7] Yet another issue relates to the setting of actual achievements with respect to the elements of the HDI against (potential) 'deprivation'. By this measure, the achievements of a poor developing country are hopelessly pitted against what the world would be like if certain ideal conditions prevailed—for instance, if the average life-expectancy was seventy-six years, the literacy 100 per cent, and the incomes very high. In other words, according to this achievement measure, developing countries would have done well *only* if they were developed countries! But notwithstanding these and other problems with the HDI, the point is that efforts are being made—though not all of them in the right direction—to remedy the perceived defects of the original development paradigm.

An important philosophical clarification needs to be made at this point. While economic development, in the last analysis, enlarges people's capabilities to choose freely from a larger menu, such freedom is also neither *absolute* nor simply *negative*. (See Chapter 5.) Instead, it is *relative* to the extent that the fruits of economic growth cannot be monopolized by only a privileged few to the exclusion of the majority of the population. Then, development economics would also negate the Nozickian 'entitlement' principle (1974) that 'what we have we hold', which advocates an essentially *negative* view of individual freedom. Instead, individual freedom should more properly be seen as *positive* in the sense that it is not just a matter of respecting some legal *procedures,* but that it also entails a duty (on the part of the individuals and the state) to prevent the undesirable social consequences of the exercise of one's individual freedom. For instance, if feudal structures get strengthened in the process of economic growth, it is not a matter of unconcern for the policy-maker or the development economist.[8] The process of economic development is much wider in scope, involving more than the protection of individual liberty as an *absolute* value. Liberty and freedom are more in the nature of instrumental values which ensure that the economic freedom for a few is translated, *through the development process, into a freedom for all, especially for the members of the least-privileged classes in the society.*

Growth and Distribution

To run the engine of growth ever faster, the founding fathers did not focus adequately on the question of an equitable re-distribution of income and wealth. Their reluctance can be attributed to an excessive faith in the 'trickle-down' effects of growth—a faith attributed to the alleged success of the Industrial Revolution in raising labour's share in total output by raising real wages. But such a simplistic belief in the trickle-down effect was questioned soon by Baran (1952), Prebisch (1959) and Myrdal (1956), among others. They highlighted the forces that limit the size of the trickle-down effect or the 'spread-effect'.

There is a consensus now that economic growth can come about with either less inequality or more of it, but this reali-zation has sunk very slowly into development thinking.[9] Kuznet's hypothesis, which predicts rising inequalities in the early stage of growth, sparked off a series of cross-country studies—for example, those by Adelman and Morris (1973), Papanek and Kyn (1986) and by Ahluwalia (1976)—which tend to test the U-shaped relationship between growth and distribution. Kuznet's hypothesis is generally supported, but with the caveat that the relationship may be the accident of history (U-shaped) or the outcome of specific policies (J-shaped).

Not only has the distributional problem been investigated thoroughly, but research has also been done on the ways and means of correcting the de-equalizing biases of growth. One approach has been to reorient the production structure in a labour-intensive way so that employment can grow faster and raise real wages, especially those of unskilled labour. Leontief (1983) conjectures that such a sequence explains the relatively more equitable industrial growth in Europe in the nineteenth century. (See Chapter 2.) In our own times, Japan and South Korea are the principal examples of such a growth strategy, which seeks to minimize the trade-off between growth and equity. [Chow and Papanek's study (1981) on Hong Kong is in the same vein; see also the *World Development Report* (1991)]. Another route to enhance the distributional content of growth is to devote an increasing proportion of the increments in national income to the provision of basic needs [Streeten et al. (1981)], or to the creation of assets owned by the poor [Chenery (1975)]. In contrast to this 'incrementalist' approach, there are others which focus on the creation of assets for the poor even *before* growth takes place [Adelman 1978)]. An important aspect of the problem is that the people's evaluation of their well-being is essentially a relative matter, because they relate their welfare to their location relative to the mean [van Praag et al. (1978)]. Thus, any successful programme of redistribution must ensure that structural reforms aimed at a redistribution of assets are carried out, and that steps are taken at the same time to ensure that the rate of increase of the income of the poor is always kept higher than the rate of increase of the income of the rich [Naqvi and Qadir (1985)].

The Question of Sectoral Balance

An important, though unfortunate, fall-out of the original

development model was the development of industry at the expense of agriculture. For instance, Lewis's two-sector model looks at agriculture as home to the 'unlimited supplies of labour', which must be drawn on to serve as an input into industrial production. Not only labour but also capital would flow to the industrial sector from the agricultural sector to provide the basis for a sustained capital accumulation and accelerated economic growth.[10] The Fei-Ranis model (1963) popularized the 'extractive' view of agriculture—as a self-sacrificing provider of inputs for economic growth. Such a forced concept of agriculture, emphasizing extraction from it rather than assigning it a positive role with a personality of its own, was mainly responsible in the late fifties and early sixties for agricultural stagnation and increasing rural poverty in the developing countries.

A vast literature has emphasized a dynamic linkage between sectors, especially that between the agriculture sector and the manufacturing sector. The main contributions have been by Ruttan-Hayami (1970), Johnston-Mellor (1961), Mellor-Johnston (1984), and Mellor (1986). The central point of these and other contributions to the area is that they consider both the contributory role of agriculture to economic development and the factors which lead to the modernization and growth of the agricultural sector itself.[11] Among such factors, technological change figures prominently—and 'naturally' because, as Schultz (1964) pointed out, continuing investments in traditional technologies are quickly thwarted by diminishing (marginal) returns. Helped by an 'endogenous' technological change, agricultural growth increases food output; and, by the same token, enlarges the size of the market for urban output. This enlargement of the market takes place by increasing the real income of the rural poor, by generating rural employment and lowering food prices through technological change.[12]

Labour Markets in Developing Countries

Another unfortunate consequence of the original development model is the rather simplistic view of the labour market
in developing countries—that labour commands very low, or
even zero, wages in the agricultural sector because of an
unlimited supply. Thus, in this model, the scattered, non-
unionized labour migrates unidirectionally from the rural
backwaters to the urban 'growth poles', where they will
hopefully be fully employed. Indeed, this aspect of development economics—that labour's marginal product is zero in
agriculture—was used (mistakenly) by Schultz (1964) to
deny the very existence of development economics.[13]

Such a simplistic view is clearly unsatisfactory. It has pro-
voked a large amount of literature examining the peculiarities
of the labour market in developing countries in general, and of
the rural market in particular.[14] The research in this area has
been helped by the advances made by micro-economic
theory about the information and risk problems, by the
availability of better and larger data on the labour markets
in developing countries, and by learning from the objective
reality in these countries. Kalecki (1971) and Mellor (1986)
show that a rising real wage plays a critical role in expanding
the size of the market for industrial goods. Another important
theoretical contribution in this area is the Harris-Todaro
model (1970), which has been generalized by Khan (1980).
The point of this study is to explain urban unemployment,
and to analyse the consequences of policies in order to reduce
it. In the model, the rural wage is determined competitively
but the urban wage is set institutionally and is typically
higher than the rural wage, which starts Lewis's process of
rural-urban migration in the *hope* (measured by the relevant
probability) of finding (full) employment in the urban sector.
Is this hope fulfilled? We may remember that Lewis said
'yes' but Harris-Todaro say 'no'—because of the labour

market distortion caused by an institutionally set urban wage, which is typically too high.[15] Does it help, then, to provide a wage subsidy to cure the urban unemployment problem? No, because it only increases the number of the urban unemployed by attracting rural labour in the *expectation* of finding more employment there. It is interesting to note that the Harris-Todaro model, rooted in the realities of the developing countries, not only corrects a defect in the original development paradigm but also one in the neo-classical model, which conjures up the myth of permanent market-clearing in the labour market—shown by Malinvaud (1984) as an untenable hypothesis even in the developed countries.

Endogenizing Demography

Another example of a creative intellectual response is to endogenize the demographic variables, such as, fertility, age-composition and migration. We know that, in the age of the (classical) 'magnificent dynamics', population was treated as an endogenous variable: Malthus treated it as one.[16] An example is the wage-fund theory wherein any attempt to improve the worker's lot by increasing wages will only be rewarded by an increase in labour supply, which will in turn reduce wages, and vice versa, if wages are reduced below the subsistence level. By the time of Lewis's work, however, population had come to be regarded as an exogenous variable. It was treated as such in the Harrod (1939)-Domar (1957) model, which, as we have noted, influenced both development theory and practice.[17] Lewis did note that population growth would lower the rate of return per capita on capital formation and would slow down the rate of absorption of labour in the urban sector. Coale and Hoover (1958) also confirmed this conjecture: a higher population growth would lower savings and capital formation.

The next step is to study the effect of economic factors (for instance, an increase in income) on population growth.[18] Coale (1973), in explaining the determinants of fertility, duly emphasizes the role played by the economic factors—namely, the decision to produce more (less) children is an integral part of household decision-making, and of the couple having a clear understanding of the advantages flowing from having a smaller family. (The third technical factor is the supply of contraceptives.) The explicit inclusion of these economic factors is an example of 'internalizing' the fertility decisions within the calculus of household decision-making. If the parents do not do so, they may desire more children than is socially desirable, and the converse as well. Here is an example of externality—that is, of market failure—because, in the absence of the possibility of making profits, the information regarding contraceptives may not be made available by the 'market'; consequently, it is a case where government intervention can prove useful.

More explicit on this are the fertility models of Becker (1960) and Mincer (1962) which include the activities of child-bearing and child-rearing as optimizing decisions taken by households. Then, attempts have been made to measure the effects of the family income and income distribution, labour force participation, and wages on fertility behaviour [Kelly (1980)]. Some modelling activity has also gone on—for example, there is Bachue's model—to relate the economic and the demographic variables.[19]

ON FARING FORWARD [20]

Let us now move on to those areas where the development economist's response has been weak and muddle-headed, and to those cases where a lot remains to be done to complete the task of creating a new paradigm of development economics, a science rich in empirical content which predicts novel facts about the real world, and is, at the same time, more fully embedded in the metaphysical environment of the developing countries. Some of these matters have been discussed in the preceding chapters, but certain aspects need more careful thought.

The Markets versus the Government

The development paradigm discussed above, especially as it was formulated by Rosenstein-Rodan (1943), Nurkse (1953), Scitovsky (1954), and Hirschman (1958), did imply government intervention to take care of incidents of market failure, or of markets which are too far from perfect or too thin, or which simply do not exist. In the absence of a strong role for international trade, due to the alleged export elasticity pessimism, coordinated investment decisions need to be taken to maximize output by taking advantage of intra-industry and intra-sector complementarities. This is the case where investment decisions are required to be taken simultaneously to secure a structure of outputs corresponding to the structure of income elasticities of demand (Nurkse's 'balanced growth' doctrine), or when, due to the shortage of investible resources, investment must be undertaken sequentially to achieve a balanced production structure only gradually (Hirschman's 'unbalanced growth' doctrine). In both these cases, the profit-maximizing private producers are not likely to optimize output because of the presence of externalities, that is, as output expands for one firm, its output-raising consequences for other firms cannot be (fully) internalized, which, in turn, prevents market prices from summarizing the information required by the private investor to maximize output. Of course, if individual firms could have complete information about the strategic responses of the other firms, then profit-seeking behaviour could do the job.

State intervention might be only of the indicative type [Scitovsky (1987)], when the market for such information does not exist, or because it is too costly or fragmentary, or where comparative advantage unfolds itself only with the passage of time. It may be more comprehensive when the strategy of investment emphasizes, as in India under the influence of Mahalanobis (1953), the priority of capital goods-producing heavy industries to facilitate the development of downstream industries—partly for non-economic reasons like defence or national pride. But there is no evidence of the development economists going for an all-out *étatisme*. In fact, the 'mixed-economy' model was preferred to the socialist (communist) model. For instance, in Pakistan and India, the founding fathers explicitly rejected both the (unalloyed) capitalist model and the communist model. With the government engaged actively in economic activities, the productive and the complementary role of the private sector has been duly accepted to the extent that it is forthcoming. And even when it does not come out into the open due to too much risk or uncertainty, the government has sought to establish industries with the explicit aim of selling these to the private takers, when they are ready to invest.

It is true that the government will not always succeed where the market fails, but the development experience shows that the government has succeeded splendidly in raising agricultural productivity by helping technological change through research institutes and by ensuring rising prices both to the producers and the consumers of food. Also, governments have managed to create fairly impressive infrastructures and industrial structures in most of the developing countries. If the element of success has been greater in one case (such as, South Korea) than in the other case (such as, India), the difference is attributable to the quality of government and to the political leadership in these countries—it did not necessarily hinge on the government being less dominant than the market. Indeed, Reynolds (1977) in his wide-ranging study explicitly attributes the differences in the comparative growth experiences of developing countries to the differences in the managing capabilities of various governments.

Keeping these facts in view, the critics of development economics who focus on the *dirigistic* practices in (some) developing countries appear somewhat ridiculous. They attribute the differences in the growth achievements of India and South Korea exclusively to the much greater role of the market in the latter than in the former. Such dubious empirical studies have been rationalized by the so-called 'neo-classical political economy' school. This literature, notwithstanding its mathematical elegance, suffers from some very serious defects. First, it is not logically permissible to infer, as these critics of development economics do, general 'statements' (the unambiguous superiority of the market-based solutions) from singular statements (the alleged growth experience of South Korea).[21] Second, being thoroughly empirical, some writers of this school commit the error of trying to establish the superiority of a non-existent phenomenon (free-markets in South Korea vs pervasive governments elsewhere) by comparing it with yet another non-existent situation (i.e., Pareto-optimality). Third, as if to turn the tables on everything, including commonsense, arguments have been put forward to establish the phenomenon of *(generalized)* government failures as opposed to the *(selective)* market failures that everybody else has believed in, which is again a *non-sequitur*. The fact is that the scenario of a generalized market success is sheer neo-classical romanticism.[22] Fourth, it is hard to understand what to make of such proofs in practice. Should one abolish governments altogether and leave everything to the Invisible Hand? The fact of the matter is that if the government must always fail, then there is no guarantee that the market will always succeed, especially where none exists [Arrow (1974)]. As Pack and Westphal (1986) point out, 'the factors responsible for a government's inability to intervene effectively may also preclude its following the neo-classical prescription.'

Such writings seem to rest their faith on the spirit of the times. The spirit appears to be made of the material of Friedman (1968) and Lucas (1972), whose contributions have been reviewed at length in Chapter 3. Briefly, according to this iconoclastic group, a real-world economy is essentially self-regulating and self-equilibrating—the economic agents are the profit-seeking, utility-maximizing individuals. In such a scenario, the government is both irrelevant and counter-productive. This is because the economic agents have access to all the information that the government may ever be able to lay its hands on. The government can at best hope to take these all-knowing individuals by surprise, but only very temporarily, according to the rational-expectations hypothesis, and briefly, according to the adaptive-expectations model. Typically, such individuals, by appropriately adjusting their (economic) behaviour, can defeat the government in its own court. Furthermore, there is no possibility of any social injustice occurring in such a situation because if, for example, unemployment prevails, it is due to the voluntary actions of the wage-earners themselves!

Another source of strength for the critics of development economics has been ('populist') supply-side economics, which was supposed to be the closest approximation to the neo-classical ideals, promising (in the eighties) to promote growth, productivity and savings, and to reduce the budgetary and the balance-of-payments deficits. The cure-all for serving such a tall order is to implement a sharp scaling down of the top marginal tax rates, which would stimulate the economy enough to yield substantially *greater* tax revenue yields (at the lower tax rates), which would then (nearly) balance the budget. Another idea, reinforcing the expansionary effect of the proposed tax cut, is due to Laffer, according to whom labour tends to work harder on finding after-tax real wage incomes rising.

What is the evidence to support these somewhat off-the-cuff ideas? The supply-side economists do not give any empirical evidence, only a list of conjectures, which is highly unsatisfactory because the economics they invented was meant to be translated into policy. The record shows that the economic effects of the 'half-baked ideas' of supply-side economics have been just the opposite of what it intended to achieve. Thurow (1990) shows that (in the U.S.) as a direct result of such policies, economic growth has stalled, savings are lower, productivity is slower, budgetary deficits have touched record highs, and the country has slipped from the position of a net creditor worth $ 141billion in 1981 to that of a net debtor of $620 billion in 1989.[23] The equity record of the supply-side economics is no better: the income differential between the rich and the poor has increased substantially in the last decade, partly because of a sharp reduction in the size of the welfare transfer payments made to reduce inflation and increase industrial productivity.

The Development Economics of Supply and Demand

The (original) development model has been described as demand-oriented and also as supply-oriented. Indeed, Lewis (1954) himself made the supply-side considerations prominent by viewing the availability of fixed capital as the main constraint on growth. In view of the (allegedly) low supply elasticities, he did not assign any significant role to demand-management policies. Thus, for instance, the Keynesian remedy of increasing the effective demand to cure unemployment in a developing country would only be penalized by greater inflation. It was thus contended that, instead of leaning on the Keynesians, the development economist should learn at the feet of classical economists (especially Ricardo) because of their emphasis on capital accumulation and a greater supply of savings as crucial factors in the development process. But, as noted by Syrquin (1988), the dynamic version of the Keynesian (Harrod-Domar) model, the two-sector Lewis model (1954), and the balanced growth model of Rosenstein-Rodan (1943) and Nurkse (1954), are, more appropriately, instances of greater emphasis on the demand-side factors.

However, it is better to think of development economics as an economics both of supply and demand—just as all economics is. While physical (and human) capital accumulation continues to be the constraining factor on growth, the inadequacy of effective demand, especially among the rural poor, also limits the growth of output and employment. This is brought out most clearly in the case of famine caused not by the short supply of food but a failure of the 'exchange entitlements' of the poor [Sen (1981)]. This argument can also be reversed: the growth-promoting impulses emanating from the demand-side will not fructify into higher levels of output (and employment) if the supply elasticities are not high enough.

Economists, including development economists, too easily forget the Marshallian scissors, with both a supply blade and a demand blade, that we need to cut anything economic. Klein [(1978), (1983)] has reformulated the problem as one of linking up the Keynesian income-and-product accounts (the demand-side),[24] the Leontief input-output framework (the supply-side) and the flow of funds accounts (the financial-side) to get a complete picture of the economic universe and to devise and implement policies on both the supply and the demand sides of the equation. It is necessary to have such a comprehensive analytical framework to analyse the effects on the economy of an increase in the prices of food, energy, and the costs associated with protecting the environment, controlling population growth, and increasing agricultural output. Such information is needed for policy-making in the developed countries as well, but it is much more pressing in the developing countries. There is an 'educative' aspect to such an exercise which is also very important. The vast data requirements for building such systems lead to a further strengthening of the data-base required for development policy. Many developing countries, including Pakistan, already have medium-sized macro-econometric models and fairly disaggregated input-output tables, and attempts are also being made to build financial flow-of-funds accounts. The next step, by no means a technically easy one to take, should also be taken. Here, 'Klein's advice (1978) is apt: 'It is wise for the development economist to be forearmed with a full model for analysis of both supply and demand sides.'

Mixing Economics with Ethics

There is, however, a more controversial issue which is actually the most fundamental problem facing economists in general, and the development economists, in particular. It is to synthesize economics with a set of universally-held ethical norms of behaviour in the society. Such a step is necessary if only because it is the most natural and realistic thing to do— natural and realistic because ethical considerations mingle with economic compulsions 'effortlessly' at the level of man's (even the economic 'agent's') primary motivation, which then translates into social action. Indeed, in the real world, the plurality of motivations is the rule rather than the exception, and we would be hard put to prove that either mere self-interest or pure altruism explains a large enough segment of social or individual action.[25] And yet mainstream

171

economics—and development economics even more so—
has remained strictly positivistic. The original development
model had no place for 'warm hearts'. By making economic
growth (the GNP) the sole maximand, and making it exclusively a function of physical capital accumulation, there is
not much room left for ethical considerations. Recent efforts
to fill in the many gaps in that model also do not come to
grips with the ethical question. If the attempts to make
development economics conform to the neo-classical prescription of cold-blooded market-oriented efficiency succeed, our discipline will become even more amoral than it already is.[26]

What influences, then, explain this neglect of ethics?
Perhaps, once again, the spirit of the times, indeed the spirit
that has moved economists since the time of Smith (1776), a
professor of moral philosophy who pronounced the separation
of economics from ethics, a separation formalized later by
Robbins (1932) into a divorce. More recently, Stigler (1981)
has laid down: 'Economists seldom address ethical questions
as they impinge on economic theory or economic behaviour.'
This is because man is 'eternally a utility-maximizer, in his
home, in his office—be it public or private—in his church, in
his scientific work, in short, everywhere.' Proceeding in the
same vein, he adds: 'Let me predict the outcome of systematic
and comprehensive testing of behaviour in situations where
self-interest and ethical values with wide verbal allegiance
are in conflict. Much of the time, most of the time in fact,
the self-interest theory (as I interpret it on Smithian lines)
will win.'

These matters have been discussed at length in the preceding chapters, especially in Chapters 5 and 6, but it may be
appropriate to briefly recapitulate. The point of departure
for extending the development economists' problematic is to
reject the Pareto-optimality principle as an operational principle. The reason is that this positivistic rule is distributionally

neutral; indeed, it is also essentially status quoist by construction. This is because *it cannot even distinguish the rich from the poor,* which is a consequence of the utilitarian and welfarist 'nature' of the principle, and also because it does not allow interpersonal comparisons of utility. As the non-utility indicators of welfare are not admissible to the utilitarian framework, the income levels enjoyed by the rich and the poor can also not provide a basis for setting up a scheme for redistributing income to the poor. But economic development, to make any sense at all, must be concerned with distributional matters.

What else is there, then, for the development economist to draw on from contemporary economic thought? The answer is, quite a lot. For instance, as noted at several points in the preceding chapters, the public-choice theory provides an excellent source for thinking about such matters. [See, for instance, Sen (1987).] In place of the Benthamite utilitarianism and the principle of Pareto-optimality, which are the central tenets of neo-classical theory, the one most relevant for development economics is a modified Rawlsian principle (1985) of 'justice-as-fairness', which would involve maximization of the welfare of the least-privileged in the society, with the explicit proviso that the number of persons so situated is minimized at the same time. An attractive feature of the Rawlsian rule is that it explicitly stipulates a *change* of the existing social order if it is not consistent with the prevalent notion of justice as fairness.

Another idea that the development economist must reject is the Nozickian non-consequentialism, with a strictly procedural and negative view of human freedom. In this view, state intervention is allowed only to prevent everyone from interfering with the entitlements of those who pass the test of procedural formalities, but no such intervention is allowed to prevent anyone from the exercise of his (legal) freedom even if that has extremely adverse consequences for the rest of the society. The state is also not allowed to intervene to redistribute income and wealth, which again is seen as an infringement of individual liberties. It should be obvious that such views cannot be of any use in a typical developing country, where redistribution is the essence of the development process.

THE REGIMEN OF POSSIBILITIES

Finally, the following remarks in this section are meant to put the discussion in this and the preceding chapters in a wider perspective. As should be clear by now, there can be no question about the 'existence' of development economics, if only one looks at the lively debate that has raged on matters which the original development model did or did not highlight. The fact that some elements of the development model—such as, the balanced or unbalanced growth doctrines and the excessive elasticity pessimism leading to the relative neglect of international trade—have fallen into disuse does not mean that development economics as a sub-discipline has ceased to be useful because of any growing incapacity to generate new ideas (which are being generated). It is only that the discipline has entered a new cycle of advancement to explain better the phenomenon of development.

There are problems with the original development model, due to Lewis and many others, but the important thing is that development economics at the time of its birth did constitute a 'paradigm-change'—namely, it shifted the focus of scientific enquiry from steady-state solutions, characterized by a constant growth in per capita incomes, to the central development concern about the causes of rising per capita incomes. (See Chapter 1.) The development paradigm involved asking many new questions, and, even more importantly, led to scientific explorations in altogether new directions, including a critical re-examination of those aspects which it featured prominently—labour surplus in agriculture, the low mobility of factors, price-inelastic demands, export pessimism and others. Indeed, many ideas of development economics have found their way into the mainstream literature, such as the Harris-Todaro conjecture which explains the pheno- menon of urban unemployment and the cost-benefit analysis apparatus designed to appraise the social profitability of investment projects [Stern (1989)]. It shows that development economics is by no means the black hole of the economic universe. Especially in response to the objective realities in developing countries, some areas of knowledge—for instance, economic demography, economic anthropology—are more relevant there than in the developed countries.

As we, the development economists, think about designing a new paradigm, it is essential that we have a critical look at our 'heritage,' which is admittedly defective—but, then, which heritage is perfect? While we do this, we must not give up the 'mixed economy' aspect of the development paradigm and its ethical foundations. The heated debate about the ills that government must bring about is based neither on good logic nor on a solid empirical base. Rivlin (1987) in her Presidential Address before the American Economic Association said: '... the arguments among economists about the merits of larger vs smaller govern- ments too often revolve around anecdotes or, worse, mis- leading statistics quoted out of context.' Needless to say, the development process itself may lead developing countries to rely increasingly on the market, but this is neither to dis- credit development economics nor to offer a prescription for embracing unalloyed capitalism, nor yet does it provide an excuse for social irresponsibility.

The new-found love of the free market that we hear so much about these days is not exclusively motivated by a concern for human freedom. Instead, as Hirschman (1988) has suggested, it is more like a *reaction* against the twentieth-century extension of the idea of citizenship in the social and the economic spheres. The main theoretical plank of this reaction is an extreme case of the (Hayekian) principle of the 'unintended social consequences of individual action', or the 'perverse reaction' principle. According to this extremist formulation, every step taken by the government to improve the lot of human beings, especially of the poor, *must* always have the perverse effect of worsening it! Such a view of human nature—that man is simply unable to make correct decisions under conditions of uncertainty—is both unscientific and contrary to facts. The fact of the matter is that individuals do learn by doing things —perhaps the wrong way at first, and that they do acquire in the process the capacity to forecast with a reasonable degree of accuracy. If this were not so, econometricians would have long gone out of business. Similarly, it would be incorrect to deny the government's ability to produce the intended effects of its decisions on economic variables because such an assertion would contradict facts; and because, to quote Hirschman (1988), 'policy-making is a repetitive, incremental activity'.

That ideas do influence human lives, for good or for evil, is illustrated best by the rapidity with which reactionary 'liberal' thought has spread all over the world. Armed with no more dangerous a weapon than the power of a basically incorrect idea repeated infinitely, the so-called liberalist philosophy has, in one country after another, pulled down welfare states, promoted high unemployment rates, widened the chasm between the rich and the poor within the country, and also the gap between rich and poor countries. The developing countries, who receive the routine and compulsory advice to dismantle their governments, and give free rein to the so-called Invisible Hand (of the vested interests), are in a worse predicament.

What, we may ask, has happened in the world that social scientists, which is what economists are basically supposed to be, have become so insensitive to the issue of unemployment, to human suffering, to the widening gulf between the rich and the poor? Invariably, the answer given by the 'liberals' is that the greater efficiency gains caused by the liberalist— read supply-side—policies will be large enough to offset the deprivations suffered by the poor. The argument is then made respectable by reference to the Pareto-optimality rule, or to the 'neutrality property' that Arrow made scientifically fashionable. However convincing such arguments may be, they are definitely unhelpful because, in fact, they make society the poorer by benumbing our sense of social responsibility and by depriving us of compassion. Development economists must, therefore, resist such ideas, for development economics is nothing if it is not relevant to policy, if it is not sensitive to social suffering, and if it is not explicitly geared to raising social welfare.

Our discipline cannot afford that Olympian detachment from the real world which has, unfortunately, become the hallmark of much of neo-classical economics. The real world is much too complex to be tackled by the 'magic of the market', or be kept on-course by the 'auto-pilot approach' [Rivlin (1987)] of the (populist) supply-siders. The task of economic development is difficult enough for the Invisible Hand to handle all by itself; the task has to bring about structural changes, especially those which will break down the strongholds of the vested interests. This may sound disruptive, even anarchic, but one should not be fearful on this account because, as Whitehead (1927) observed, 'the major advances in civilization are processes which all but wreck the societies in which they occur.'[27] This is what economic transformation has done elsewhere—for example, by destroying feudal structures in the West. That epic battle must be re-enacted in the developing countries as well if we hope to crown the development effort with success.

NOTES

[1]For example, the principle that the size of the agricultural surplus and the availability of foreign exchange determine the size of the non-farm population; the concept of gains from trade; the distinction between tradeables and non-tradeables; the determination of net saving out of profit rather than wages; and a significant promotional role for the government.

[2]This is a Popperian methodological ploy (1980), advocated by Friedman (1953), and one that is now widely accepted by (mainstream) economists.

[3]As Solow (1988) points out, '... it is an implication of the diminishing returns that the equilibrium rate of growth is not only not proportional to the saving (investment) rate, but is independent of the saving (investment) rate.'

[4]Lewis (1955) laid down: 'First, it should be noted that our subject-matter is growth, and not distribution.' Among the pioneers, Tinbergen is perhaps the sole exception to the pervasive insensitivity to distributional issues.

[5]However, Tinbergen's optimum regime (1959) emphasized not only the objectives of economic development but also the policy instruments to achieve them optimally—not merely the growth of key inputs, as advocated by Lewis and others, but also distributive justice.

[6]Sen (1983); Lewis (1984); Stern (1989); and most recently a two-volume *Handbook of Development Economics* [Chenery and Srinivasan (1988), (1989)] has been published by North Holland, which runs to the impressive length of 1773 pages. It includes comprehensive surveys in as many as thirty-two areas, including such important matters as trade and development, fiscal policy, project evaluation, processes of structural transformation, migration and urbanization, and the economics of health, nutrition and education, to name only a few. An extensive bibliography is appended to each of the surveys.

[7]Difficulties also arise because the Gini Coefficients do not correctly reflect the state of income distribution when the 'coverage' of the Income and Expenditure Surveys used for computing the Ginis is as limited as it is in most developing countries. For instance, in Pakistan's Household Income and Expenditure Survey for 1984-85 more than 99.9 per cent of the households reported a monthly income *from all sources* no more than Rs 0.18 million, which is much below the average income of the top income group in Pakistan. (The highest tax bracket for super tax is of Rs 50 million per annum, which itself is a gross underestimation.) Thus, an apparently adverse movement in the Gini Coefficient may simply mean

a greater concentration of income in the hands of middle-class families as reflective of the dynamics of economic development.

[8]Considerations like those noted in the text militate against the point of view that economic development can be left entirely to the magic of the market precisely because individual liberty 'is best preserved in a regime that allows markets a major role' [Buchanan (1986)].

[9]Based on the 1970 census, Fishlow (1972) found that, in Brazil, notwithstanding—or, perhaps, as a result of—the high growth rates, income inequalities grew bigger, with the poor losing out even in *absolute* terms.

[10]Hirschman (1958) also supported a subservient role for agriculture in the growth process. He wrote: 'Agriculture certainly stands convicted on the count of its lack of direct stimulus to the setting up of few activities through linkage effects—the superiority of manufacture in this respect is crushing.'

[11]Johnston and Mellor (1961) wrote: 'It is our contention that balanced growth is needed in the sense of simultaneous efforts to promote agricultural and industrial development.'

[12]Note an important point here: in this view, higher food output is secured by lowering—instead of by raising—food prices. This is because continuously rising food prices would *contract* the size of the market by reducing the real income of the rural poor, who spend an overwhelming proportion of their income on food.

[13]This view is mistaken because, as noted by Bell (1987), all that is required for the validity of the Lewis model is that the urban sector attract rural labour at a *constant* real wage. This constancy may, in turn, be ensured by population growth, greater women participation in the labour force and other such factors.

[14]See Rozenzweig (1989) for a useful review of the literature on this topic.

[15]The *unemployment* equilibrium condition in this model is denoted by the equality of the rural wage to the expected urban wage.

[16]But in so far as Malthus treated population as a geometrically increasing function of time, the population variable is really exogenous in his model as well.

[17]Looking back, it is somewhat ironical that Lewis, notwithstanding his many intellectual journeys back in time to 'visit' Adam Smith, Malthus, and Mill, did not notice this aspect of the classical growth model.

[18]This work, both theoretical and empirical, has been well summarized in Birdsall (1988).

[19]Another pioneering study of this kind—linking household fertility decisions with income and expenditure, labour force participation, and rural-urban migration—has also been completed at the Pakistan Institute

of Development Economics. The study shows that the two-way link between the economic and the demographic variables is significant.

[20]'Not fare well/But fare forward, voyagers.' (*The Dry Salvages* by T.S. Eliot.)

[21]As Popper (1980) points out, the only valid procedure is to empirically test theories after they have been advanced, not the other way round.

[22]It is generally forgotten that market success is guaranteed *only* if there are enough markets, if both the consumers and producers behave competitively, and if equilibrium exists, and that non-satisfaction of *any* of these conditions to a withdrawal of the guarantee of market success. [See Debreu (1959)].

[23]According to the latest re-estimation done by the U.S. Department of Commerce, the result quoted in the text holds even if re-evaluated at today's *market* prices; even though the extent of indebtedness is much less.

[24]Klein is careful to note that the income-and-product accounts include some very important supply-side elements as well.

[25]As Solow (1980) pointed out, without positing some kind of ethical norms of behaviour it is not possible, for example, to explain why sometimes the labour market is *not* self-clearing, 'Wouldn't you be surprised if you learned that someone of roughly your status in the profession, but teaching in a less desirable department, had written to your department chairman offering to teach your courses for less money?' Normally, the answer would be in the affirmative: yes, I would be damned surprised if someone did this to me or to you. Although it may not be the economically optimal situation, it would be most desirable that someone did *not* undercut me or you.

[26]It is interesting to note in this context that the two-volume *Handbook of Development Economics* [Chenery and Srinivasan (1988), (1989)] does not include any separate review of the literature on the subject—because there is not much available on the subject! Only Sen (1988), at the beginning of the *Handbook,* talks about some of his own work on the subject—mostly relating to his 'capability' theory—but this discussion does not produce any ripples in the positivist analyses in the remaining 1,700-plus pages! The same is true of the most recent survey of literature by Stern (1989).

[27]Quoted in Hirschman (1988).

References

ADELMAN, IRMA (1978), *Redistribution Before Growth: A Strategy for Developing Countries,* Inaugural Lecture for the Cleveringa Chair, Leiden University, The Hague: Martinus Nijhof.

—— and CYNTHIA T. MORRIS (1973), *Economic Growth and Social Equity in Developing Countries,* Stanford, Calif: Stanford University Press.

AHLUWALIA, MONTEK S. (1976), 'Inequality, Poverty, and Development', *Journal of Development Economics,* 6, 307-342.

AKERLOF, G. (1970), 'The Market for Lemons,' *Quarterly Journal of Economics,* August, 488-500.

AMIN, SAMIR (1976) ,*Unequal Development,* Sussex: Harvester Press.

ARROW, KENNETH J. (1974), 'Limited Knowledge and Economic Analysis', *The American Economic Review,* 61:1, 1-10.

—— (1977), 'Current Developments in the Theory of Social Choice, *Social Research,* 44:4, 607-622.

—— (1979),'The Property Rights Doctrine and Demand Revelation under Incomplete Information', in Michael J. Boskin (ed.),

Economics and Human Welfare: Essays in the Honor of Tiber Scitovsky, New York: Academic Press Inc., 23-39.

BALASSA, BELA (1971), *The Structure of Protection in Developing Countries,* Baltimore: The Johns Hopkins University Press.

BARAN, PAUL (1952), 'On the Political Economy of Backwardness', *Manchester School.*

BARDHAN, PRANAB (1988), 'Alternative Approaches to Development Economics', in Hollis Chenery and T.N. Srinivasan (eds.), *Handbook of Development Economics:1,* Oxford:North-Holland, 39-71.

BATOR, Francis M. (1958) 'The Anatomy of Market Failure,' *'The Quarterly Journal of Economics,* 72:3, 351-379.

BAUER, PETER T. (1972), *Dissent on Development: Studies and Debates in Development Economics,* Cambridge, Mass: Harvard University Press.

—— (1984) *Reality and Rhetoric: Studies in the Economics of Development,* Cambridge, Mass: Harvard University Press.

—— (1984a), 'Remembrance of Studies Past: Retracing First Steps,' in Gerald M. Meier and Dudley Seers (eds.), *Pioneers in Development,* New York: Oxford University Press (for the World Bank).

BECKER, GARY S. (1960), 'An Economic Analysis of Fertility,' in Universities—National Bureau Committee for Economic Research (ed.), *Demographic and Economic Change in Developed Countries,* Princeton, N.J.: Princeton University Press.

—— (1962), 'Investment in Human Capital: A Theoretical Analysis', *The Journal of Political Economy,* 70:5 (Part 2), 9-49.

—— (1964), *Human Capital: A Theoretical and Empirical Analysis with Special Reference to Education,* New York: National Bureau of Economic Research and Columbia University Press.

—— (1983), 'A Theory of Competition among Pressure Groups for Political Influence', *The Quarterly Journal of Economics,* 97:3, 371-400.

BELL, CLIVE (1987), 'Development Economics', in John Eatwell, Murray Milgate and Peter Newman (eds.), *The New Palgrave: A Dictionary of Economics, I:(A-D),* London: Macmillan.

BELL, DANIEL, and IRVING KRISTOL (1981), *The Crisis in Economic Theory,* New York: Basic Books, Inc.

BERRY, R. ALBERT and WILLIAM R. CLINE (1979), *Agrarian Structure and Productivity in Developing Countries,* Baltimore: The Johns Hopkins University Press.

BHAGWATI, JAGDISH N. (1968), 'Distortions and Immiserizing Growth: A Generalization', *Review of Economic Studies,* 35:104, 481-485.

References

BHAGWATI, JAGDISH N. (1978), *Anatomy and Consequences of Exchange Control Regime*, Cambridge, Mass: Ballinger.

—— (1982), 'Directly Unproductive Profit-seeking (DUP) Activities', *The Journal of Political Economy*, 90:5, 988-1002.

—— (1984), 'Development Economics: What have We Learned?, *Asian Development Review*, 2:1, 23-38.

—— (1985), *'Growth and Poverty'*, Occasional Paper No.5, Michigan State University, Center for Advanced Study of International Development.

—— and SUKHAMOY CHAKRAVARTY (1969), 'Contributions to Indian Economic Analysis: A Survey', *The American Economic Review*, 59:4 (Part 2), 2-73.

—— and T. N. SRINIVASAN (1982), 'The Welfare Consequences of Directly Unproductive Profit-seeking (DUP) Lobbying Activities: Prices versus Quantity Distortions', *Journal of International Economics*, 13:1/2, 33-44.

—— RICHARD A. BRECHER and T. N. SRINIVASAN (1984), 'DUP Activities and Economic Theory', in David C. Collander (ed.), *Neoclassical Political Economy: An Analysis of Rent Seeking and DUP Activities*, Cambridge: Ballinger Publishing Co., 17-32.

BINSWANGER, HANS P., and VERNON RUTTAN (1978), *Induced Innovation: Technology, Institutions and Development*, Baltimore: The Johns Hopkins University Press.

BIRDSALL, NANCY (1988), 'Economic Approaches to Population Growth', in H.B. Chenery and T. N. Srinivasan (eds.), *Handbook of Development Economics 1*, New York: North-Holland and Elsevier Science Publishers.

BLAUG, MARK (1976), 'Kuhn versus Lakatos *or* Paradigm versus Research Programmes in the History of Economics', in Spiro J. Latsis (ed.), *Method and Appraisal in Economics*, Cambridge: Cambridge University Press, 149-180.

—— (1983), *The Methodology of Economics, or How Economists Explain*, Cambridge: Cambridge University Press.

BOULDING, KENNETH (1966), 'The Economics of Knowledge and the Knowledge of Economics', *The American Economic Review*, 56:2, 1-13.

BOWLES, SAMUEL(1985), 'The Production Process in a Competitive Economy: Walrasian, Neo-Hobbesian, and Marxian Models', *The American Economic Review*, 75:1, 16-36

BRAHMANAND, P.R., and C.N. VAKIL (1956), *Planning for an Expanding Economy*, Bombay.

BRANDT, W. (1980), *North-South. A Program for Survival*, London: Pan.

Development Economics

Brock, William A., and Stephen P. Magee (1984), 'The Invisible Foot and the Waste of Nations: Redistribution and Economic Growth,' in David C. Collander (ed.), *Neoclassical Political Economy: An Analysis of Rent Seeking and DUP Activities,* Cambridge: Ballinger Publishing, 177-186.

Buchanan, Allen (1985), *Ethics, Efficiency, and the Market,* Littlefield (USA): Rowman and Allenheld.

Buchanan, James M. (1986), *Liberty, Market and State: Political Economy in 1980s,* Sussex: Wheatsheaf Books Ltd.

——— and W.C. Stubblebine (1962), 'Externality', *Economica,* 29, 371-384

——— and G. Tullock (1962), *The Calculus of Consent: Logical Foundation of Constitutional Democracy,* Ann Arbor: The University of Michigan Press.

Calabresi, G. (1968), 'Transaction Costs. Resource Allocation and Liability Rules: A Comment,' *Journal of Law and Economics,* 11, 67-73.

Cardoso, F.H. (1972), 'Dependency and Development in Latin America,' *New Left Review,* 74, 83-95.

Chakravarty, Sukhamoy (1969), *Capital and Development Planning,* Cambridge, Mass: The MIT Press.

——— (1984), 'Aspects of India's Development Strategy for the 1980s,' *Economic and Political Weekly,* 19:20 & 21, 845-852.

Chenery, Hollis B. (1965), 'Comparative Advantage and Development Policy,' in American Economic Association and the Royal Economic Society, *Surveys of Economic Theory: Growth and Development, II,* Surveys V-VIII, New York: St. Martin's Press; London: Macmillan.

——— (1975), 'The Structuralist Approach to Development Policy,' *The American Economic Review* (Papers and Proceedings), 65:2, 310-316.

——— (1983), 'Interaction between Theory and Observation in Development', *World Development,* 11:10, 853-861.

——— and T.N. Srinivasan (eds.) (1988, 1989), *Handbook of Development Economics* I&II, New York, Elsevier Science Publishers.

——— Montek S. Ahluwalia, C.L.G. Bell, John H. Duloy and Richard Jolly (1974), *Redistribution with Growth,* London: Oxford University Press.

Chow, C. Steven and Gustav F. Papanek (1981), 'Laissez-faire, Growth and Equity—Hong Kong,' *Economic Journal,* 91:362, 466-485.

Clark, Colin (1984), 'Development Economics: The Early Years,' in Gerald M. Meier and Dudley Seers (eds.), *Pioneers in Development,* New York: Oxford University [for the World Bank.]

References

COALE, A. J. (1973), Demographic Transition Reconsidered. *Proceedings,* Leige: The International Union for Scientific Study of Population.

—— and EDGAR M. HOOVER (1958), *Population Growth and Economic Growth in Low Income Countries,* Princeton, N.J.: Princeton University Press.

COASE, R.H. (1960), 'The Problem of Social Cost,' *Journal of Law and Economics,* 3, 1-44.

COHEN, SULEIMAN I.(1978), *Agrarian Structures and Agrarian Reform,* Leiden/Boston: Martinus Nijhoff.

—— (1980), 'Two Attempts to Extend Economic Model to Socio-political Issues and Realities,' *The Pakistan Development Review,* 24:4, 281-310.

COLLANDAR, DAVID C. (1984), *Neoclassical Political Economy: The Analysis of Rent-seeking and DUP Activities,* Cambridge, Mass: Ballinger Publishing Co.

CORDEN, W.M. (1966), 'The Structure of a Tariff System and Effective Protection Rate,' *The Journal of Political Economy,* 74:3, 221-237.

CORNWALL, JOHN (1977), *Modern Capitalism: Its Growth and Transformation,* London: Martin Robertson.

CROOK, CLIVE (1989), 'The Third World: Trial and Error: Poor Man's Burden,' *The Economist,* 23-29 September.

DAHRENDORF, RALF (1989), 'Liberalism,' in John Eatwell, Murray Milgate and Peter Newman (eds.), *The Invisible Hand (The New Palgrave),* London: Macmillan.

DEANE, PHYLLIS (1983), 'The Scope and Method of Economic Science,' *Economic Journal,* 93:369, 1-12.

DEBREU, GERARD (1959), *Theory of Value: An Axiomatic Analysis of Economic Equilibrium,* Cowles Foundation, Monograph No. 17, New York: Wiley.

—— (1987), 'Mathematical Economics', in John Eatwell, Murray Milgate and Peter Newman (eds.), *The New Palgrave: A Dictionary of Economics, (K-P),* London: Macmillan, 399-403.

—— (1991), 'The Mathematization of Economic Theory,' *The American Economic Review,* 81:1, 1-6.

DENISON, EDWARD F. (1962), *The Sources of Economic Growth in the United States and the Alternatives before US,* New York: Committee for Economic Development.

—— (1967), *Why Growth Rates Differ: Post-War Experience in Nine Western Countries,* Washington, D.C.: Brookings Institution.

—— (1985), *Trends in American Growth, 1929-1982,* Washington, D.C.: Brookings Institution.

Development Economics

DOMAR, EVSEY D. (1946), 'Capital Expansion, Rate of Growth, and Employment', *Econometrica*, 14, 137-147.

—— (1957), *Essays in the Theory of Economic Growth*, Westport, C.T.: Greenwood.

DUESENBERRY, JAMES (1952), *Income, Saving and Theory of Consumer Behavior*, Cambridge, Mass: Harvard University Press.

EMMANUEL, ARGHIRI (1972), *Unequal Exchange: A Study of the Imperialism of Trade*, New York and London: Monthly Review Press.

FEI, JOHN C.H. and GUSTAV RANIS (1963), 'Innovation, Capital Accumulation and Economic Development', *The American Economic Review*, 53:3, 283-313.

FINDLAY, RONALD (1979), 'Economic Development and the Theory of International Trade', *The American Economic Review*, 69:2, 186-190.

—— (1988), 'Trade, Development and the State', in Gustav Ranis and T. Paul Schultz (eds.), *The State of Development Economics*, New York: Basil Blackwell, 78-95.

FISHLOW, ALBERT (1972), 'Brazilian Size Distribution of Income,' *The American Economic Review*, 62, 391-402.

FRIEDMAN, MILTON (1953), *Essays in Positive Economics*, Chicago: University of Chicago Press.

—— (1968), 'The Role of Monetary Policy,' *The American Economic Review*, 58:1, 1-17.

FURUBOTN, EIRIK G., and SVETOZAR PEJOVICH (1972), 'Property Rights and Economic Theory: A Survey of Recent Literature,' *The Journal of Economic Literature*, 10:4, 1137-1162.

GALENSON, WALTER, and HARVEY LEIBENSTEIN (1955), 'Investment Criteria, Productivity, and Economic Development,' *The Quarterly Journal of Economics*, 69:3, 343-370.

GERSCHENKRON, ALEXANDER (1962), *Economic Backwardness in Historical Perspective: A Book of Essays*, Cambridge, Mass : Harvard University Press.

GILDER, GEORGE (1981), *Wealth and Poverty*, New York: Basic Books.

GOODWIN, R.M. (1990), *Chaotic Economic Dynamics*, Oxford: Oxford University Press, p. 198.

GRAAFF, J. DE V. (1989), 'Social Cost,' in John Eatwell, Murray Milgate and Peter Newman (eds.), *The Invisible Hand. (The New Palgrave)*, London: Macmillan.

GRIFFIN, K.B., and J.L. ENOS (1970), 'Foreign Assistance: Objectives and Consequences', *Economic Development and Cultural Change*, 18:3, 313-327.

HABERLER, GOTTFRIED (1980), *Notes on Rational and Irrational Expectation*, Report No. III, Washington, D.C: American Enterprise Institute.

References

HABERLER, GOTTFRIED (1988), *International Trade and Economic Development* (with a new Introduction), San Francisco: International Center for Economic Growth.

HAHN, F.H. (1987), 'Neo-classical Growth Theory,' in Eatwell, Milgate and Newman, *The New Palgrave: A Dictionary of Economics*, 3: (K-P), London: The Macmillan Press Ltd.

HAQ, MAHBUB UL (1963), *The Strategy of Economic Planning: A Case Study of Pakistan*, Karachi: Oxford University Press.

HARE, R.M. (1963), *Freedom and Reason*, Oxford: Oxford University Press.

HARRIS, JOHN R., and MICHAEL P. TODARO (1970), 'Migration, Unemployment and Development: A Two-sector Analysis,' *The American Economic Review*, 60:1, 125-142.

HARROD, R.F. (1939), 'An Essay in Dynamic Theory,' *Economic Journal*, 49:193, 14-33.

——— (1970), *Towards a Dynamic Economics: Some Recent Developments of Economic Theory and their Application to Policy*, London: Macmillan.

——— (1972), *The Life of John Maynard Keynes*, London: Penguin Books (first published in 1951).

HARSANYI, JOHN C. (1977), 'Morality and the Theory of Rational Behaviour,' *Social Research*, 44:4, 623-656.

——— (1977a), *Rational Behaviour and Bargaining Equilibrium in Games and Social Situations*, Cambridge: Cambridge University Press.

HAYEK, F.A. (1960), *The Constitution of Liberty*, London: Routledge and Kegan Paul.

HEILBRONER, ROBERT (1990), 'Analysis and Vision in the History of Modern Economic Thought,' *Journal of Economic Literature*, 28:3, 1097-1114.

HICKS, JOHN (1965), *Capital and Growth*, New York: Oxford University Press.

——— (1976), 'Revolution in Economics', in Spiro J. Latsis (ed.), *Method and Appraisal in Economics*, London: Cambridge University Press (reprinted in 1978), 207-218.

HIRSCHMAN, ALBERT O. (1958), *The Strategy of Economic Development*, New Haven, Conn: Yale University Press.

——— (1981), *Essays in Trespassing: Economics to Politics and Beyond*, Cambridge: Cambridge University Press.

——— (1981a), 'Morality and the Social Sciences: A Durable Tension,' in Albert O. Hirschman (ed.), *Essays in Trespassing: Economics to Politics and Beyond*, Cambridge: Cambridge University Press.

Development Economics

HIRSCHMAN, ALBERT O. (1981*b*), 'The Rise and Decline of Development Economics,' in Albert Hirschman (ed.), *Essays in Trespassing: Economics to Politics and Beyond*, Cambridge: Cambridge University Press.

—— (1984), 'A Dissenter's Confessions: The Strategy of Economic Development Revisited,' in Gerald M. Meier and Dudley ʒers (eds.), *Pioneers in Development*, New York: Oxford University Press (for the World Bank).

—— (1988), 'Two Hundred Years of Reactionary Rhetoric: The Case of the Perverse Effect,' in Grethe B. Peterson (ed.), *The Tanner Lectures on Human Values*, X, 1989, Salt Lake City: University of Utah Press.

—— and MICHAEL ROTHSCHILD (1973), 'Changing Tolerance for Income Inequality in the Course of Economic Development (with a Mathematical Appendix),' *The Quarterly Journal of Economics*, 87:4, 544-566.

IQBAL, MOHAMMAD (1986), *The Reconstruction of Religious Thought in Islam*, Lahore: Institute of Islamic Culture.

JOHNSON, HARRY G. (1969), 'The Theory of Effective Protection and Preferences,' *Economica*, 36:142, 119-139.

JOHNSTON, BRUCE F. and JOHN W. MELLOR (1961), 'The Role of Agriculture in Economic Development,' *The American Economic Review*, 51:4, 566-593.

JONES, L.P. and I. SAKONG (1980), *Government, Business and Entrepreneurship in Economic Development: The Korean Case*, Cambridge, Mass: Harvard University Press.

KALDOR, NICHOLAS (1955), 'Alternative Theories of Distribution,' *Review of Economic Studies*, 23.

KALECKI, M. (1971), *Selected Essays on the Dynamics of the Capitalist Economy*, Cambridge: Cambridge University Press.

KELLY, A.C. (1980), 'Interactions of Economic and Demographic Household Behaviour', in R.A. Easterlin (ed.), *Population and Economic Change in Developing Countries*, Chicago: University of Chicago Press.

KEMP, MURRAY C. and MICHIHIRO OHYAMA (1978), 'On the Sharing of Trade Gains by Resource-poor and Resource-rich Countries,' *Journal of International Economics*, 8:1, 93-115.

KENDRIK, J.W. (1961), *Productivity Trends in United States*, Princeton: Princeton University Press.

KEYNES, JOHN M. (1936), *The General Theory of Employment, Interest and Money*, New York: Harbrace.

KHAN, M. ALI (1979), 'Relevance of Human Capital Theory to Fertility Research: Comparative Findings for Bangladesh and Pakistan,' in Ismail Sirageldin (ed.), *Research in Human Capital and Development:* 1, Greenwich, Conn.: JAI Press Inc.

KHAN, M. ALI (1980), 'The Harris-Todaro Hypothesis and the Heckscher-Ohlin-Samuelson Trade Model: A Synthesis, *Journal of International Economics,* 10:4, 527-548.

―――― (1980a), 'Dynamic Stability, Wage Subsidies and the Generalized Harris-Todaro Model,' *The Pakistan Development Review,* 19:1, 1-24.

―――― (1987a), 'Harris-Todaro Model,' in *The New Palgrave: A Dictionary of Economics, 2: (E to J),* London: Macmillan, 592-594.

―――― (1987b) 'Perfect Competition,' in J. Eatwell, M. Milgate and P.K. Newman (eds.), *The New Palgrave: A Dictionary of Economics, 3 (K-P),* New York: Macmillan.

―――― (1989), ' In Praise of Development Economics,' *The Pakistan Development Review,* (Papers and Proceedings), 28:4 (Part I), 337-378.

――――― (1991), 'On the Languages of Markets,' *The Pakistan Development Review,* 30:4 (Part I), 503-545.

―――― and Y. SUN (1990), 'On a Reformulation of Cournot-Nash Equilibria,' *Journal of Mathematical Analysis and Application,* 146,442-460.

KHAN, MAHMOOD HASAN (1975). *The Economics of the Green Revolution in Pakistan,* New York: Praeger Publishers.

―――― (1983), 'Classes and Agrarian Transition in Pakistan,' *The Pakistan Development Review,* 22:3, 129-162.

KLAMER, ARJO (1984), *The New Classical Macro-economics: Conversations with the New Classical Economists and their Opponents,* Sussex: Wheatsheaf Books Ltd.

KLEIN, LAWRENCE R.(1978), 'The Supply Side,' *The American Economic Review,* 68:1, 1-7.

―――― (1983), *The Economics of Supply and Demand,* Oxford: Basil Blackwell.

―――― (1985), 'Reducing Unemployment without Inflation,' *America,* 4 May, 362-365.

KOOPMANS, T.C. (1957), *Three Essays on the State of Economics Science,* New York: McGraw-Hill.

KREPS, D. (1990), *Micro-economic Theory,* Princeton, N.J.: Princeton University Press.

KRISHNA RAJ (1963), 'Farm Supply Response in India-Pakistan: A Case Study of the Punjab Region', *Economic Journal,* 73:3, 477-487.

KRUEGER, ANNE O. (1974), 'The Political Economy of the Rent-seeking Society', *The American Economic Review,* 64:3, 291-303.

―――― (1978), *Liberalization Attempts and Consequences,* Cambridge. Mass: Ballinger.

KUHN, THOMAS (1962), *The Structure of Scientific Revolutions*, Chicago: University of Chicago Press.

KUZNETS, SIMON (1955), 'Economic Growth and Income Inequality', *The American Economic Review*, 45:1, 1-28.

—— (1971), *Economic Growth of Nations: Total Output and Production Structure*, Cambridge, Mass: Harvard University Press.

LAFFONT, J.J. (1984), 'Externalities,' in John Eatwell, Murray Milgate, and Peter Newman (eds.), *The Invisible Hand (The New Palgrave)*, London: Macmillan.

LAKATOS, IMRE (1970), 'Falsification and Methodology of Scientific Research,' in Imre Lakatos and A. Musgrave (eds.), *Criticism and Growth of Knowledge*, Cambridge: Cambridge University Press.

LAL, DEEPAK (1983), *The Poverty of 'Development Economics'*, London: Institute of Economic Affairs, Hobart Paperback 16.

LEIBENSTEIN, HARVEY (1957), *Economic Backwardness and Economic Growth*, New York: John Wiley.

LEONTIEF, WASSILY (1983), 'Technological Advance, Economic Growth and the Distribution of Income,' *Population and Development Review*, 9:3, 403-410.

LEWIS, W. ARTHUR (1954), 'Economic Development with Unlimited Supplies of Labour', *Manchester School*, 22, 139-191.

—— (1955), *The Theory of Economic Growth*, London: Unwin University Press.

—— (1980), 'The Slowing Down of the Engine of Growth,' *The American Economic Review*, 70:4, 555-564.

—— (1984), 'The State of Development Theory,' *The American Economic Review*, 74:1, 1-10.

—— (1984a), 'Development Economics in the 1950s,' in Gerald M. Meier and Dudley Seers (eds.), *Pioneers in Development*, New York: Oxford University Press (for the World Bank).

—— (1988), 'The Roots of Development Theory,' in H. B. Chenery and T. N. Srinivasan (eds.), *Handbook of Development Economics*, 1, New York: Elsevier Science Publishers, 27-37.

LEWIS, STEPHEN R., Jr. (1969), *Economic Policy and Industrial Growth in Pakistan*, London: Allen and Unwin.

LITTLE, IAN M. D. (1982), *Economic Development: Theory, Policy, and International Relations*, New York: Basic Books.

LUCAS, ROBERT E., Jr. (1972), 'Expectations and Neutrality of Money,' *Journal of Economic Theory*, 4, 103-124.

—— and THOMAS SARGENT (1978), 'After Keynesian Macroeconomics',

References

in *After the Phillips Curve: Persistence of High Inflation and High Unemployment*, Boston: Federal Reserve Bank of Boston, 49-72.

LUCE, R. D. and H. RAIFFA (1958), *Games and Decisions*, New York: John Wiley.

MACHLUP, FRITZ (1956), 'Rejoinder to a Reluctant Ultra-empiricist', *Southern Economic Journal*, 22, 483-493.

MAHALANOBIS, P.C. (1953) 'Some Observations on the Process of Growth of National Income', *Sankhya*, 12:4, 307-312.

MALINVAUD, EDMOND (1969), 'Capital Accumulation and Efficient Allocation of Resources,' first published in *Econometrica*, 1953, reprinted in Kenneth J. Arrow and T. Scitovsky (eds.), *Readings in Welfare Economics*, London: George Allen and Unwin, 645-681.

——— (1984), *Mass Unemployment*, New York: Basil Blackwell.

MARSHALL, T.H. (1950), *Citizenship and Social Class*, Cambridge: Cambridge University Press.

MARX, KARL (1959), *Capital: The Communist Manifesto*, New York: The Modern Library (reprint).

MEADE, JAMES (1983), 'Impressions of Maynard Keynes,' in D. Worswick and D. Trevithick (eds.), *Keynes and the Modern World*, Cambridge: Cambridge University Press.

MEIER, GERALD M. (1984), *Emerging from Poverty: The Economics that Really Matters*, New York: Oxford University Press.

MELLOR, JOHN W. (1986), 'Agriculture on the Road to Industrialization,' in John P. Lewis and V. Kallab (eds.), *Development Strategies Reconsidered*, USA: Transaction Books [for Overseas Development Council].

——— and BRUCE F. JOHNSTON (1984), 'The World Food Equation: Inter-relations Among Development, Employment and Food Consumption,' *Journal of Economic Literature*, 22:2, 531-574.

MILIBAND, R. (1983), 'State Power and Class Interests,' *New Left Review*, 138.

MINCER, J. (1962), 'Market Prices, Opportunity Costs, and Income Effect.' in C. Christ *et al.* (eds.), *Measurement in Economics: Studies in Mathematical Economics and Econometrics in Memory of Yehuda Grenfeld*, Stanford: Stanford University Press.

MODIGLIANI, FRANCO (1977), 'The Monetarist Controversy, or Should We Forsake Stabilization Policies', *The American Economic Review*, 67:2, 1-19.

MORRIS, M. D. (1979), *Measuring the Condition of the World's*

Poor: The Physical Quality of Life Index, New York: Pergamon Press.

MUELLER, DENNIS C. (1979), *Public Choice,* Cambridge: Cambridge University Press.

MUSGRAVE, R. A. (1959), *The Theory of Public Finance,* New York: McGraw-Hill.

MYRDAL, GUNNAR (1956), *Development and Underdevelopment,* Cairo: National Bank of Egypt.

—— (1956*a*), *An International Economy: Problems and Perspectives,* Westport, Conn: Greenwood Press.

—— (1984), 'International Inequality and Foreign Aid in Retrospect,' in Gerald M. Meier and Dudley Seers (eds.), *Pioneers in Development,* New York: Oxford University Press [for the World Bank].

NAQVI, SYED NAWAB HAIDER (1969), 'Protection and Economic Development,' *KYKLOS,* XXII.

—— (1981), *Ethics and Economics: An Islamic Synthesis,* Leicester: The Islamic Foundation.

—— (1982), 'The "Policy Gaps", Allocative Inefficiencies and Self Reliance,' in Heinz Ahrens and Wolfgang Peter Zingel (eds.), *Towards Reducing the Dependence on Capital Imports,* Weisbaden: Franz Steiner Verlag.

—— et al. (1983), *The P.I.D.E. Macro-econometric Model of Pakistan's Economy,* 1, Islamabad: Pakistan Institute of Development Economics.

—— and ASGHAR QADIR (1985), 'Incrementalism and Structural Change: A Technical Note', *The Pakistan Development Review,* 24:2, 87-102.

—— and ATHER MAQSOOD AHMED (1986), *Preliminary Revised P.I.D.E. Macro-econometric Model of Pakistan's Economy,* Islamabad: Pakistan Institute of Development Economics.

—— and PETER A. CORNELISSE (1986), 'Public Policy and Wheat Market in Pakistan', *The Pakistan Development Review,* 25:2, 99-126.

——, MAHMOOD HASAN KHAN and M. GHAFFAR CHAUDHRY(1989), *Structural Change in Pakistan's Agriculture,* Islamabad: Pakistan Institute of Development Economics.

—— and A. R. KEMAL (1991), *Protectionism and Efficiency in Manufacturing: A Case Study of Pakistan,* San Francisco, California: ICS Press.

NORTH, D. (1984), 'Three Approaches to the Study of Institutions,' in David C. Collander (ed.), *Neoclassical Political Economy: The Analysis of Rent Seeking and DUP Activities,* Cambridge, Mass: Ballinger, 33-40.

References

NOZICK, ROBERT (1974), *Anarchy, State, and Utopia*, Oxford: Basil Blackwell.

NURKSE, RAGNAR (1953), *Problems of Capital Formation in Underdeveloped Countries*, New York: Oxford University Press.

OHLIN, P.G. (1959), 'Balanced Economic Growth in History,' *The American Economic Review* (Papers and Proceedings), 49:2, 338-353.

OKHAWA, K., B. F. JOHNSTON and H. KANEDA (eds.) (1970), *Agriculture and Economic Growth: Japan's Experience*, Princeton, N. J.: Princeton University Press.

OLSON, M., Jr. (1965), *The Logic of Collective Action: Public Goods and the Theory of Groups*, Cambridge, Mass: Harvard University Press.

PACK, HOWARD, and LARRY E. WESTPHAL (1986), 'Industrial Strategy and Technological Change: Theory versus Reality', *Journal of Development Economics*, 22:1, 87-128.

PAPANEK, GUSTAV F. (1967), *Pakistan's Development: Social Goals and Private Incentives*, Cambridge, Mass: Harvard University Press.

——— (1972), 'The Effect of Aid and other Resources on Savings and Growth in Less Developed Countries,' *Economic Journal*, 82:327, 934-950.

——— and OLDRICH KYN (1986), 'The Effect of Income Distribution of Development, the Growth Rate, and Economic Strategy,' *Journal of Development Economics*, 23:1, 55-66.

PASTORAL LETTER ON CATHOLIC SOCIAL TEACHING AND THE U.S. ECONOMY (1985), Washington, D. C.: National Conference of Catholic Bishops.

PERROUX, F. (1955), 'Note on the Notion of Poles of Growth' (French), *Economie Appliquee*, 8, Series D, Jan-June.

PIGOU, A. C. (1932), *The Economics of Welfare*, London: Macmillan.

POPPER, KARL R. (1980), *The Logic of Scientific Discovery*, first published in English in 1959, London: Hutchinson, tenth (revised) impression.

PREBISCH, RAUL (1950), *The Economic Development of Latin America and Its Principal Problems*, New York: The United Nations, Department of Economic Affairs.

——— (1959), 'Commercial Policies in Underdeveloped Countries', *The American Economic Review*, 49:2, 251-273.

——— (1984), 'Five Stages in My Thinking on Development,' in Gerald M. Meier and Dudley Seers (eds.), *Pioneers in Development*, New York: Oxford University Press [for the World Bank].

PUTNAM, H. (1990), *Realism with a Human Face*, Cambridge, Mass: Harvard University Press.

RAWLS, JOHN (1971), *A Theory of Justice,* Cambridge, Mass : Harvard University Press/Oxford: Clarendon Press.

—— (1985), 'Justice as Fairness: Political not Metaphysical', *Philosophy and Public Affairs,* 14:3, 223-251.

REYNOLDS, LOYD G. (1977), *Image and Reality in Economic Development,* New Haven, Conn.: Yale University Press.

RIVLIN, ALICE M. (1987), 'Economics and the Political Process', *The American Economic Review,* 77:1, 1-10.

ROBBINS, LIONEL (1932), *An Essay on the Nature and Significance of Economic Science,* London: Macmillan.

ROBINSON, JOAN (1979), *Aspects of Development and Underdevelopment,* Cambridge: Cambridge University Press.

ROSENSTEIN-RODAN, P. N. (1943), 'Problems of Industrialization of Eastern and South-eastern Europe', *Economic Journal,* 53:210, 202-211.

—— (1984), 'Natura Facit Saltum: Analysis of Disequilibrium Growth Process,' in Gerald Meier and Dudley Seers (eds.), *Pioneers in Development,* New York: Oxford University Press [for the World Bank].

ROSTOW, W. W. (1956), 'The Take-off into Self-Sustained G owth,' *Economic Journal,* 66.261, 25-48.

—— (1971), *Stages of Economic Growth,* Cambridge: Cambridge University Press, second edition.

ROZENZWEIG, MARK R. (1989), 'Labour Markets in Low-Income Countries,' in Hollis B. Chenery and T.N. Srinivasan (eds.), *Handbook of Development Economics,* 1, New York: Elsevier Science Publishers.

RUTTAN, VERNON W. (1982), *Agricultural Research Policy,* Minneapolis: University of Minnesota Press.

—— and YUJIRO HAYAMI (1970), 'Factor Prices and Technical Change in Agricultural Development: The United States and Japan 1880-1960,' *The Journal of Political Economy,* 78:5, 1115-1141.

SAMUELSON, PAUL A. (1966), 'A Brief Survey of Post-Keynesian Development,' in Joseph E. Stiglitz (ed.), *The Collected Scientific Papers of Paul A. Samuelson,* II. Cambridge. Mass: MIT Press. 1534-1550.

—— (1969), 'Pure Theory of Public Expenditure and Taxation,' in J. Margolis and H. Guitton (eds.), *Public Economics,* New York: St. Martin's Press.

—— (1976), *Economics,* New York: McGraw-Hill, tenth edition.

SARGENT, THOMAS J. and NEIL WALLACE (1975), ' "Rational" Expectations, the Optimal Monetary Instruments and the Optimal Money Supply Rule,' *The Journal of Political Economy,* 83:2, 241-254.

References

SATO, R. (1963), 'Fiscal Policy in a Neo-classical Growth Model: An Analysis of Time Required for Equilibrating Adjustment,' *Review of Economic Studies*, 30:82, 16-23.

SCHULTZ, THEODORE W. (1962), 'Reflections on Investment in Man,' *The Journal of Political Economy*, 70:5 (Part 2), 1-8.

——— (1964), *Transforming Traditional Agriculture*, Chicago: The University of Chicago Press.

——— (1970), *Investment in Human Capital: The Role of Education and Research*, New York: Macmillan and Free Press.

——— (1981), 'The Economics of Being Poor' in Theodore Schultz (ed.), *Investing in People: The Economics of Population Quality*, Berkeley and Los Angeles: University of California Press.

——— (1981a), *Investing in People: The Economics of Population Quality*, Berkeley and Los Angeles: University of California Press.

SCHUMPETER, JOSEPH A. (1934), *The Theory of Economic Development*, Cambridge, Mass: Harvard University Press.

SCITOVSKY, TIBOR (1954), 'Two Concepts of External Economies', *The Journal of Political Economy*, 17:2, 143-151.

——— (1987), 'Balanced Growth' in John Eatwell, Murray Milgate and Peter Newman (eds.), *The New Palgrave: A Dictionary of Economics*, I:(A-D).

SEN, AMARTYA K. (1967), 'Surplus Labour in India: A Rejoinder of Schultz's Test', *Economic Journal*, 77: 305 (March), 163-165.

——— (1970), 'The Impossibility of the Paretian Liberal,' *Journal of Political Economy*, 78, 152-157, reprinted in A. K. Sen (1983), *Choice, Welfare and Measurement*, Oxford: Basil Blackwell, 285-290.

——— (1970a), *Collective Choice and Social Welfare*, San Francisco: Holden-Day Inc.

——— (1979), 'Personal Utilities and Public Judgements: Or What's Wrong with Welfare Economics?', *Economic Journal*, 89:355, 537-558.

——— (1981), *Poverty and Famine: An Essay on Entitlement and Deprivation*, Oxford: Clarendon Press.

——— (1981a), 'Public Action and the Quality of Life in Developing Countries,' *Oxford Bulletin of Economics and Statistics*, 43:4, 287-319.

——— (1983), 'Development: Which Way Now?', *Economic Journal*, 93:372, 745-762.

——— (1983a), 'Equality of What?' in A. K. Sen, *Choice, Welfare and Measurement*, Oxford: Basil Blackwell, 353-369. First published in *Tanner Lectures on Human Values*, 1 (1980).

SEN, AMARTYA K. (1983*b*), 'Poverty: An Ordinal Approach to Measurement,' in A. K. Sen, *Choice, Welfare and Measurement*, Oxford: Basil Blackwell, 373-387.

—— (1984), *Resources, Values and Development*, Oxford: Basil Blackwell.

—— (1985), Review of Kenneth J. Arrow's *Social Choice and Justice*, *Journal of Economic Literature*, 23:4, 1764-1776.

—— (1987), *On Ethics and Economics*, Oxford: Basil Blackwell.

—— (1988), 'The Concept of Development,' in H. B. Chenery and T. N. Srinivasan (eds.), *Handbook of Development Economics*, 1, New York: Elsevier Science Publishers.

SHAPIRO, CARL and JOSEPH E. STIGLITZ (1984), 'Equilibrium Unemployment as a Worker Discipline Device', *The American Economic Review*, 74:3, 433-444.

SIDGWICK, H. (1874), *The Methods of Ethics*, London: Macmillan.

SIMON, HERBERT A. (1983), *Reason in Human Affairs*, Oxford: Basil Blackwell.

SINGER, HANS W. (1950), 'The Distribution of Gains between Investing and Borrowing Countries', *The American Economic Review*, (Papers and Proceedings), 40:2, 473-485.

—— (1952), 'The Mechanics of Economic Development', *Indian Economic Review*, 1.

SIRAGELDIN, ISMAIL (1966), *Non-market Components of National Income*, Ann Arbor: University of Michigan.

—— (1979), 'United Nations/UNFPA Export Group Meeting on Demographic Transition and Socio-economic Development,' in *Demographic Transition and Socio-economic Development*, with United Nations Secretariat, the United Nations Department of International Economic and Social Affairs, Population Studies, No. 65, 5-30.

——, JAMES MORGAN and NANCY BAERWALDT (1966), *Productive Americans*, Ann Arbor: Survey Research Center, University of Michigan.

SKINNER, ANDREW S. (1989), 'Adam Smith' in John Eatwell, Murray Milgate, Peter Newman (eds.), *The Invisible Hand: The New Palgrave*, London: Macmillan.

SMITH, ADAM (1975), *An Enquiry into the Nature and Causes of the Wealth of Nations*, reprinted by R. H. Campbell and A. S. Skinner, Oxford: Clarendon Press (originally published in 1776).

SOLOW, ROBERT M. (1957), 'Technical Change and the Aggregate Production Function,' *Review of Economic and Statistics*, 39:3.

—— (1980), 'On Theories of Unemployment,' *The American Economic Review*, 70:1, 1-11.

References

SOLOW, ROBERT M. (1988), 'Growth Theory and After,' *The American Economic Review*, 78:3, 307-317.

SPRAOS, J. (1980), 'The Statistical Debate on the Net Barter Terms of Trade between Primary Commodities and Manufactures,' *Economic Journal*, 90, 107-128.

SRAFFA, PIERRO (1975), *Production of Commodities by Means of Commodities*, London: Cambridge University Press.

STERN, NICHOLAS (1989), 'The Economics of Development: A Survey', *The Economic Journal*, 99:397, 597-685.

STIGLER, GEORGE J. (1965), 'The Economist and the State', *The American Economic Review*, 55:1, 1-18.

—— (1981), 'Economics or Ethics?' in Sterling McMurrin (ed.), *Tanner Lectures on Human Values*, II, Cambridge: Cambridge University Press, 145-191.

STIGLITZ, JOSEPH E. (1988), 'Economic Organization' Information, and Development', in H. Chenery and T. N. Srinivasan (eds.), *Handbook of Development Economics*, 1, New York: North Holland.

STREETEN, PAUL (1959), 'Unbalanced Growth,' *Oxford Economic Papers*, 11:2, 167-190.

—— (1980), 'Basic Needs in the Year 2000,' *The Pakistan Development Review*, 19:2, 129-141.

—— et al. (1981), *First Things First: Meeting Basic Human Needs in the Developing Countries*, New York: Oxford University Press [for the World Bank].

SYRQUIN, MOSHE (1988), 'Patterns of Structural Change' in Hollis B. Chenery and T. N. Srinivasan (eds.), *Handbook of Development Economics*, Amsterdam: North-Holland, 203-273.

TEMKIN, LARRY S. (1986), 'Inequality,' *Philosophy and Public Affairs*, 15:2, 99-121.

THUROW, LESTER C. (1983), *Dangerous Currents: The State of Economics*, London: Oxford University Press.

—— (1990), 'How Supply-side Myths Warp the Political Process,' *International Herald Tribune*, Paris, 10 October.

—— (1990a), 'The Supply-side Destination is a Frail Plutocracy', *International Herald Tribune*, Paris, 11 October.

TINBERGEN, JAN (1959), 'The Theory of Optimum Regime,' in L. H. Klassen, L. M. Kyock and J. H. Witteveen (eds.), *Jan Tinbergen: Selected Papers*, Amsterdam: North-Holland, 264-304.

—— (1977) *On the Theory of Economic Policy*, Amsterdam: North-Holland.

—— (1982), 'Ways to Socialism,' *Coexistence*, 19:1.

197

Development Economics

TINBERGEN, JAN (1985), *Production, Income and Welfare: The Search for an Optimal Social Order*, Brighton, Sussex: Wheatsheaf Books.

TOBIN, JAMES (1985), 'Unemployment, Poverty and Economic Policy,' *America*, 4 May, 359-362.

TULLOCK, GORDON (1986), *The Economics of Wealth and Poverty*, Brighton, Sussex: Wheatsheaf Books.

UNDP (1990), *Human Development Report, 1990*, New York: Oxford University Press [for UNDP].

UNDP (1991), *Human Development Report, 1991*, New York: Oxford University Press [for UNDP].

VAN PRAAG B., T. GOEDHART and A. KAPTEYN (1978), *The Poverty Line: A Pilot Survey in Europe*, Leiden: Centre for Research in Public Economics, Leiden University.

VEBLEN, THORSTEIN B. (1973), *The Theory of the Leisure Class: With an Introduction by John Kenneth Gabraith*, London: Houghton.

WALTERS, ALAN A. (1989), in J. Eatwell et al. (eds), *Economic Development*, London: Macmillan Press, 59-60.

WHITEHEAD, ALFRED. N. (1927), *Symbolism: Its Meaning and Effect*, New York: Capricorn Books.

WICKSELL, K. (1958), 'A New Principle of Just Taxation,' reprinted in R. A. Musgrave and A. T. Peacock (eds.), *Classics in the Theory of Public Finance*, New York: Macmillan.

WORLD BANK (1982), *World Development Report 1982*, New York: Oxford University Press [for the World Bank].

——— (1986), *Poverty and Hunger*, Washington, D.C.: The World Bank.

——— (1991), *World Development Report 1991: (The Challenge of Development)*, New York: Oxford University Press.

YOTOPOULOS, PAN A. (1985), 'Middle-Income Classes and Food Crises: The New Food-Feed Competition,' *Economic Development and Cultural Change*, 33:3, 463-483.

——— (1989), 'The (Rip) Tide of Privatization: Lessons from Chile,' *World Development*, 17:5, 683-702.

Index

199

Index

Naqvi, 66n; and Kemal, 41; and Qadir, 67n, 160
Naqvi et al., 27n, 37, 46n
neo-classical economics, 16, 17, 21, 30, 39, 43, 64, 100, 107, 108, 116, 146, 177; the Akerlof–Stiglitz version of, 26n; growth model, 54, 67n; growth theory, 26n
neo-classical political economy, 137; advocates of, 74; the emergence of, 63; school, 167; vision, 23
neo-Keynesian, 76–77, 80
neo-Keynesian consensus, the dissolution of, 75–82
neo-mercantilist, 61
neutral property, 177
new-old religion, the emergence of, 51–52
Nigeria, 67n
nihilism, 79, 80, 90
non-consequentialism, 20, 100, 114, 115, 126, 173
non-consequentialist moral-rights theories, 117, 120, 124–25, 126
normative judgements, 16, 20, 21, 91, 92, 141, 145
North, 137
North–South dialogue, virtual collapse of, 9
Nozick, 99, 114, 115, 122, 123, 124; entitlement principle, 114–16, 125, 158; non-consequentialism, 20, 100, 115, 173
Nurkse, 33, 56, 71, 72, 105, 165; balanced growth doctrine, 151, 165, 170

Ohlin, 152
Okhawa et al., 66n
Olson, 90
optimal control, the theory of, 16
optimal tax-cum-subsidy policies, 74
organization (socialist) scheme, a Lange–Lerner type of, 131
'ought questions', 20

Pack and Westphal, 147n, 168

Pakistan, 15, 27n, 41, 67n, 81, 115, 132; economic policy in, 49–52; feudal-capitalistic structures in, 37; Household Income and Expenditure Survey (1984–85), 178n
(The)Pakistan Development Review, 24
Pakistan Institute of Development Economics, 179n
Papanek, 66n, 67n; and Kyn, 159
'paradigm shift', 36
Paretian philosophy, 99
Pareto-efficient solution, 130, 131, 132, 134, 136, 137
Pareto-optimality principle, 10, 17, 18, 20, 21, 25, 27n, 41, 44, 88, 100, 103n, 109, 110, 112, 124, 126, 129–34, 138–42, 146, 147n, 167, 172, 173, 177; as a collective-choice rule, 92–95; the distributive neutrality of, 27n
Pastoral Letter, 27n
pecuniary externality, 102n
Perroux, theory of unbalanced growth, 55
perverse reaction principle, 176
Petty, William, 150
Philippines, 27n
Phillips curve, 78
philosophy of science, the methodology of, 35
Physical Quality Index (PQLI), 157
Pigou, 56; on market failure, 89
pioneers-latecomers' syndrome, 22, 33
policy-maker(s), 47, 48, 49–52, 53, 60, 61, 65, 73, 79, 81, 106, 159
political action programme (PAP), 63
Popper, 35, 180n
Popperian methodological ploy, 178n
population growth, 43, 171; the effect of economic factors on, 164; high rates of, 82
poverty, 20, 22, 24, 42, 49, 57, 59, 102, 110, 113, 141; alleviation of, 16; the intensity of, 81; the

205

Index

self-interest maximization rule, 20, 27n, 108, 109, 111, 125, 126

self-interest theory, 172

self-policing competition, 130, 131

Sen, A.K., 25, 26n, 31, 44, 48, 66n, 67n, 68n, 84, 88, 95, 103n, 110, 116, 127n, 139, 147, 148n, 150, 170, 173, 178n, 180n; basic capability equality, 143, 145; concept of capabilities, 125; Impossibility Theorem, 140; study of famines, 156; theory of entitlement, 59–60

Shapiro and Stiglitz, 135

Simon, 85

Singapore, 48

Singer, 34

Sirageldin, Ismail, 25, 42

Skinner, 127n

Smith, Adam, 32, 46n, 48, 62, 65n, 66n, 88, 91, 96, 121, 172, 179; automatic price mechanism run by invisible hand, 42, 43; on market failure, 91–92; *Theory of Moral Sentiments*, 109; *The Wealth of Nations,* 150

social choice theories, 126

Social Indicators of Development (SID), 26n

social justice, 10, 38, 101, 102

social organization, 83, 108

Solow, 37, 59, 80, 154, 155, 178n, 180n

South–east Asia, 14

South Korea, 15, 27n, 38, 48, 66n, 132, 133, 167

Soviet Union, 14, 15

spontaneous order/coordination, principle of, 91

Spraos, 35

Sraffa's generalization of the Ricardian theory of determination of the rate of profit on investment, 38

Srinivasan, 63, 74

standard economic theory, 30, 32, 36, 39, 40, 44

state intervention, 10, 18, 34, 51, 63, 129, 132, 133, 166, 173; a denuncia-

tion of, 41; the form and mechanics of, 90; *see also* government intervention

status quoist, 17, 21, 112, 173

steady-state growth path, 36, 150, 151, 152

Stern, 31, 175, 178n

Stigler, 19, 173

Stiglitz, 26n

Streeten, 57; humanism, 57, 58

Streeten et al., 160; the basic-needs approach, 157

structural change, 18, 19, 27n, 37, 38, 41, 57, 59, 64, 65, 67n, 72, 84, 107, 113, 120, 121, 177; the attempts at, 60; the problems of, 82

structural transformation, 54, 67n, 141, 146; process of, 178n

Stubblebine, 134

Suppe's grading principle, 125

supply and demand, the development economics of, 169, 171

supply side economies, 15, 23, 55, 58, 62, 84, 168, 169, 177, 180n

surplus labour theory, 45n; *see also* labour surplus

Syrquin, 170

Taiwan, 27n, 48

technological change, 17, 42, 59, 64, 84, 154, 161, 166

technological externality, 89, 102n

technological progress, 43, 59, 154

Temkin, 118, 119

Thurow, 79, 169

Tinbergen, Jan, 23, 25, 42, 43, 45, 64, 85; optimum regime, 178n

Tobin, 27n, 76, 80

total utility equality, 143

Trends in Developing Economics (TIDE), 26n

tricle-down effects, 55

Tullcok, 118, 119; on market failure, 92

unanimity principle, 92, 99, 109, 124, 141